FLIGHT

THE TRIALS AND TRIUMPHS
OF AIR PIONEERS

By
Reg Grant

Consultant
Michael Allaby

A Dorling Kindersley Book

Dorling DK Kindersley
LONDON, NEW YORK, MUNICH,
MELBOURNE, and DELHI

Project Editor Matt Turner
Project Art Editor Keith Davis
Senior Editor Fran Jones
Senior Art Editor Stefan Podhorodecki
Category Publisher Linda Martin
Managing Art Editor Jane Thomas
Picture Researcher Marie Osborn
DK Picture Library Jonathan Brookes
Production Jenny Jacoby
DTP Designer Siu Yin Ho

First published in Great Britain in 2003 by
Dorling Kindersley Limited
80 Strand, London WC2R ORL

A Penguin Company

2 4 6 8 10 9 7 5 3 1

The CIP Catalogue record for this book is available from the British Library

ISBN 0-7513-3754-4

Reproduced by Colourscan, Singapore
Printed and bound by L.E.G.O., Italy

See our complete catalogue at
www.dk.com

CONTENTS

INTRODUCTION

About a century ago, on windswept sand dunes on the Atlantic coast of the United States, Orville Wright climbed into a homemade flying machine built of wood, cloth, piano wire, and bicycle chains. Lying flat on his stomach, Orville lifted from the ground and flew for 12 seconds before coming down with a bump. And that was the beginning of aircraft flight!

Today, more than a billion people fly every year in aeroplanes that can stay airborne for hours and travel at speeds unimagined in Orville Wright's day. Astronauts venture into space and have journeyed as far as the Moon. So how did people turn the dream of flying like birds into a reality? And once airborne, how did the pioneers of flight develop the incredible aircraft that we see today?

IS IT A PLANE OR A HELICOPTER? IT'S BOTH – AN AUTOGIRO OF THE EARLY 1900S.

FAST AND HIGHLY MANOEUVRABLE, THE
F-15 JET FIGHTER HAS SERVED THE UNITED
STATES AIR FORCE FOR MORE THAN 30 YEARS.

In the search for answers to these questions, you'll
follow a story of heroic adventures – of men and
women who crossed oceans and mountain ranges in
tiny aeroplanes, or who pushed aircraft to the limits
in the search for maximum speed. You'll learn what it
was like to cruise in style in one of the great airships
that once sailed the skies, or to pilot a rocket plane
dropped like a bomb from another aircraft.

You'll also encounter some of the world's most
extreme machines, from aircraft powered by bicycle
pedals or sunlight to the mighty Saturn rocket that
propelled men on their course to the Moon.

To help you explore the subject further, there are
Log On "bites" that appear throughout the book.
These will lead you to websites where you can find
more detailed information and images.

So, fasten your
seat-belts for a
thrilling trip
through the
story of flight!

TO FLY LIKE A BIRD

Have you ever secretly wished you could simply spread your arms and flap high into the sky, just like a bird? Dreams such as this led our ancestors to invent machines that really could take to the air. From their first daring attempts in balloons and weird gliders, the passion for powered flight fast took shape.

GREEK INVENTOR DAEDALUS FLIES ON HIS FEATHERED WINGS. MADE IN 1493, THIS IS THE FIRST PRINTED IMAGE OF HUMAN FLIGHT.

Birdbrain

If you had lived in Berlin, Germany, in the late 1800s, you might have enjoyed a local attraction – the flights of the landing clumsily a few seconds later at the foot of the hill. Lilienthal was trying to fulfil an age-old human dream of flying like the birds. If they could do it, then why couldn't we?

"BIRDMAN" LILIENTHAL MADE OVER 1,000 GLIDING FLIGHTS

"birdman" Otto Lilienthal. Before an awestruck crowd, the bearded Lilienthal stood on a hill with bird-like wings fitted to his body. Then he marched downhill into the wind with his wings spread until a gust lifted him into the air. He would soar over the spectators at a height of 10–20 m (33–66 ft), before

Coming unstuck

The Ancient Greeks, for instance, had created the myth of Daedalus and Icarus. They were a father and son who tried to escape imprisonment on the island of Crete by using wings made of feathers stuck together with wax. In this ancient story, Daedalus succeeds in flying to

8

freedom, but Icarus flies too close to the Sun. The wax gluing his wings together melts, and he plunges to his death.

Despite this discouraging tale, history is full of examples of people who have tried to fly. Most fixed crude wings to their arms and jumped off a tower or a cliff. All, like Icarus, came unstuck. Those that didn't die were badly injured.

Da Vinci's dreams

Even the great Italian inventor Leonardo da Vinci imagined that a person would be able to fly by flapping wings. Da Vinci lived about 500 years ago. The flying machines he sketched in his notebooks were based on his observation of birds and bats. He also drew a kind of helicopter. But Leonardo's machines were hopeless.

The trouble was that human muscles just aren't up to flapping flight. Birds have very light bodies, and the muscles that operate their wings are incredibly powerful in relation to their size. Lilienthal showed the best that could be achieved with wings on your arms – a short downhill glide.

OTTO LILIENTHAL TAKES OFF IN ONE OF HIS EARLY FLYING EXPERIMENTS. HE WAS SURE HUMANS COULD LEARN TO FLY BY COPYING BIRDS.

9

A load of hot air

When people first did succeed in getting airborne, a little over 200 years ago, it was in a completely un-birdlike manner.

A DUCK WAS ONE OF THE WORLD'S THREE FIRST BALLOONISTS, SENT UP BY THE MONTGOLFIER BROTHERS ON A TEST FLIGHT WITH A CHICKEN AND A SHEEP.

The airmen were a couple of brothers, Joseph and Etienne Montgolfier, paper manufacturers from the French town of Annonay. They noticed that if a test flight before attempting a human ascent. Then on 21 November 1783 two brave Frenchmen, Pilâtre de Rozier and the Marquis d'Arlande, became the first people to fly. They climbed into the basket under a Montgolfier balloon

THE FUEL FOR THE FIRST HUMAN FLIGHT WAS SIMPLY DRY STRAW

you filled a paper bag with hot air by holding it over a fire, it would soar upwards. This is because hot air is lighter than cold air. The bag of hot air rises in the same way that a cork bobs back to the surface if you place it under water.

The Montgolfiers reasoned that if you had a big enough hot-air bag, or balloon, it would lift something strapped underneath it – for example, a basket with people in it.

F armyard fliers

The brothers built a series of large balloons. They sent up a duck, a chicken, and a sheep on

and rose from the ground. Feeding a fire in a straw-filled brazier to keep the bag filled with hot air, they stayed aloft for 25 minutes and travelled 8 km (5 miles) before coming safely to earth.

P opular pastime

Balloons really caught on. Hot air was soon mostly replaced by lighter-than-air gases such as hydrogen. Balloonists made some epic flights – for example, across the Channel from England to France in 1785. But the drawbacks of balloons were obvious. They were at the mercy of the weather, travelling wherever the wind blew them. And they needed a huge gas bag to carry just two or three people. Balloons were fun, but they weren't of much use.

THE MONTGOLFIERS DEMONSTRATE THEIR RICHLY DECORATED HOT-AIR BALLOON IN FRONT OF AN AWESTRUCK CROWD IN 1783.

A im high!

As the 18th century drew to a close, however, one man started thinking a little further. He was Sir George Cayley, an English country gentleman from Yorkshire. Cayley got his ideas from flying kites. He reasoned that if a balloon could carry people aloft, perhaps a kite could do the same. He tied a big kite across a pole, making the first aircraft wing. He added a movable tail to the end of the pole to make his aircraft go up and down and turn from side to side. From 1809, Cayley began testing the aircraft, which on occasion carried a small boy for a few metres.

AN "AERIAL STEAM
CARRIAGE" FLIES OVER A CITY – A FANTASY
IMAGE ADVERTISING A PROPOSED "STEAM
AIRLINE" IN 1843.

How planes fly

Cayley also published his
thoughts on heavier-than-air
flight. He explained the basic
principles of lift, thrust, and
drag. Lift is the
upward force
provided by the
wing. It has to be
sufficient to raise
the weight of the
aircraft and pilot.
Thrust, the power
driving the plane
forward, has to be
strong enough to

overcome drag – the resistance
of air to anything trying to
advance through it.

Nobody really listened to
Cayley's ideas. In any case, no
one could think of a way to
power an aircraft. Cayley's first
idea was to
propel his
machine
forwards using
oars, like a
rowing boat!

WEIRD WORLD

IN 1853, SIR GEORGE CAYLEY
MADE HIS COACHMAN FLY A
SHORT DISTANCE IN A GLIDER.
THE COACHMAN INSTANTLY
QUIT HIS JOB, TELLING
CAYLEY: "I WAS HIRED
TO DRIVE, AND NOT
TO FLY."

Winging it

Without an engine,
fliers could do no
more than glide.

Through the 1800s, countless experiments by people such as French sea captain Jean-Marie Le Bris and American engineer Octave Chanute showed how wings could be designed to increase lift. But Chanute's gliders could fly at most a few hundred metres downhill.

More hot air

During the 1800s, steam engines came into use to power railway locomotives and ships. Inventors thought of using steam to drive flying machines by turning a propeller. But steam engines were simply too heavy for flight. The most successful steam-powered flying machine was the Eole, a bat-winged design by French engineer Clément Ader.

It managed just a few seconds in the air. Practical, powered, heavier-than-air flight needed a new kind of engine.

Invented in the 1880s, petrol engines were much lighter than steam engines. They at last gave inventors a real chance of designing a flying machine that actually worked.

The Wright idea

In 1899 two brothers living in Dayton, Ohio, decided to have a go at heavier-than-air flight. They were Wilbur and Orville Wright, and they ran a bicycle shop, making and selling their own bikes.

Having read up all that had been written about flying, the Wrights built a glider in their workshop. In the summer of 1900 they took it to Kitty Hawk, a tiny settlement on the coast of North Carolina, and set up their camp in the windswept sand dunes.

THIS IS ONE OF SIR GEORGE CAYLEY'S DESIGNS FOR A MANNED GLIDER. CAYLEY KNEW IN THEORY HOW TO FLY, BUT DOING IT IN PRACTICE WAS NOT SO EASY.

Learning the ropes

The Wright brothers' approach to flying was much more practical and methodical than anyone else's. Day after day they experimented with glider

History is made

In September 1903 the Wrights took their *Flyer* to Kitty Hawk. They ran into many difficulties, though, and were almost pipped at the post in the race

flights down the dunes, working out what went wrong each time they crashed. Gradually they learned to pilot an aircraft. They worked out how to control the glider in pitch (nose up or down), in yaw (from side to side), and in roll (wings going down on one side and up on the other).

For the winter they returned to the workshop in Dayton and improved their glider in the light of their experiments. Two more summers passed at Kitty Hawk, and by 1903 the brothers were ready to fit a petrol engine to their glider

WEIRD WORLD
THIS FAMOUS PHOTO OF THE WRIGHT BROTHERS' FIRST FLIGHT WAS SHOT BY KITTY HAWK RESIDENT JOHN DANIELS, WHO HAD NEVER TAKEN A PHOTOGRAPH BEFORE.

WATCHED BY HIS BROTHER WILBUR, ORVILLE WRIGHT TAKES OFF ON THE FIRST FLIGHT AT KITTY HAWK ON 17 DECEMBER 1903.

to be first to fly. While they had been at work, Samuel Pierpoint Langley, a famous American scientist, had spent a fortune in taxpayers' money on an official project to achieve the first manned heavier-than-air flight.

Langley's large petrol-driven flying machine, the *Aerodrome*, was ready by October 1903. But launched from the top of a houseboat on the Potomac

River, it plunged straight into the water. A second attempt on 8 December failed in the same way, almost drowning the unfortunate pilot.

Over the next two years they improved their *Flyer* until they could make flights of over half an hour. It was not until 1908, when Wilbur demonstrated their aircraft to huge

This left the way open for the Wright brothers, and on 17 December 1903 they made four powered flights. The first, by Orville, lasted 12 seconds. The last, by Wilbur, covered 260 m (852 ft) in 59 seconds.

These first few powered flights are now the stuff of aviation legend, but at the time the newspapers made little fuss. This is perhaps understandable. After all, flying for less than a minute in sand dunes didn't sound great. But the Wrights knew that they had cracked it.

crowds in France, that the Wright brothers were finally credited with being the first to achieve sustained, controlled, heavier-than-air flight.

WILBUR WRIGHT TAKES A PASSENGER UP IN 1908. LADY FLIERS TIED THEIR SKIRTS AROUND THEIR ANKLES WITH STRING TO AVOID SHOWING THEIR UNDERWEAR.

UP, UP, AND AWAY

Would you have dared to fly in a rickety little plane powered by a motorbike engine? The early aviators must have had boundless courage, for the first true flying machines had a nasty habit of killing their pilots. Nevertheless, the pioneering spirit made sure there was a constant stream of pilots prepared to risk all for the glory.

LOUIS BLERIOT'S FLYING HELMET WAS A CRUDE EAR-WARMER, BUT VITAL IN AN OPEN COCKPIT.

On a wing and a prayer
Early on the morning of 25 July 1909, a man with a droopy moustache and a tight-fitting cap climbed into the seat of an aircraft in a field on the north

A THREE-CYLINDER MOTORBIKE ENGINE POWERED THE TYPE XI PLANE FLOWN BY BLERIOT IN JULY 1909.

BLERIOT'S WORRIED WIFE LATER BANNED HIM FROM FLYING

coast of France. The aviator Louis Blériot was setting out to win a £1 000 prize put up by a British newspaper for the first person to fly over the Channel to England. Although the distance was only 32 km (20 miles), it was a desperate venture in a flimsy aircraft made of wood, wire, and fabric, and powered by a crude motorbike engine.

Close call

Blériot took off and vanished into the morning mist, flying low over the sea at about 48 kmh (30 mph). He had no compass and almost missed England completely. Luckily, after about 20 minutes he spotted the white cliffs of Dover. He landed in a field near Dover castle, with a crunch that smashed the wheels on his plane.

Journey to glory

Blériot's flight, though just over 36 minutes long, caused a stir. Few people had believed that an aircraft could ever fly across water from country to country. Blériot was a hero and Europe went flight crazy.

Until the Channel crossing, flight was only of real interest to a handful of enthusiasts in Europe and the United States of America – men like Blériot himself and the Wright brothers. A month after Blériot's flight, when almost all the pilots in the world turned up for the first ever air show at Reims, in eastern France, there were a mere 22 of them.

Yet over half a million people came to see the fliers in action. There were plenty of thrills and spills – one pilot flew into a haystack – but most people were just amazed to see aircraft fly at all.

17

F lying fever
Over the next few years, hundreds of adventurous young men and women learned to fly. They

WEIRD WORLD
IN THE 1911 PARIS-MADRID AIR RACE, A CRASHING PLANE KILLED THE FRENCH MINISTER OF WAR AND INJURED THE PRIME MINISTER, WHO HAD COME TO WATCH.

A ir races
Long-distance races were staged – from London to Manchester, from Paris to Madrid,

were drawn by the excitement of flight and by the chance of fame. Huge crowds attended air shows, and excitement rose to fever pitch during record-breaking, long-distance flights by the daring aviators. These included Georges Chavez, who became the first man to fly over the Alps in 1910, and Roland Garros, who flew across the Mediterranean Sea from France to North Africa in 1913.

THOMAS SELFRIDGE WAS THE FIRST PERSON TO DIE IN AN AIR CRASH, KILLED WHEN FLYING IN A PLANE PILOTED BY ORVILLE WRIGHT ON 17 SEPTEMBER 1908.

from Paris to Rome. These were pretty chaotic events. To avoid getting lost, pilots mostly followed roads or railways. If they did lose their way,

His wife followed him by train and nursed him back to health after each crash.

LOG ON...
Learn more about
Louis at www.bleriot.com

FRENCH PILOT LOUIS PAULHAN, FLYING A FARMAN BIPLANE, IS ON HIS WAY TO WINNING THE LONDON-TO-MANCHESTER AIR RACE IN 1910. THERE WERE ONLY TWO CONTESTANTS FOR THE HEFTY PRIZE OF £10,000.

FIRST AVIATION MEETING IN ENGLAND.

CODY
DELAGRANGE
FARMAN
SOMMER
LEBLON
MOLON
PREVOT
DE LA VAUX
& OTHER
AVIATORS ENGAGED.

DONCASTER
15TH TO 23RD OCTOBER 1909.

COLOURFUL POSTERS ADVERTISED THE AIR SHOWS WHERE MOST PEOPLE CAUGHT THEIR FIRST EXCITING GLIMPSE OF AN AEROPLANE.

which happened frequently, they landed in a field and asked for directions. Often no more than two or three fliers completed the race, and the countryside was strewn with the mangled wreckage of aircraft that didn't make the distance.

In 1911 the American Cal Rodgers took up a challenge to fly across the United States from coast to coast. It took him 7 weeks and 18 crashes to get from New York to California!

S afety last
Flying was incredibly dangerous in these pioneering days. Pilots seldom wore seat-belts. Passengers either sat on the wing and held onto one of the struts, or squeezed in behind the pilot, as if they were on the back of a motorbike. All too often the engines broke down. Luckily,

19

early aircraft could glide well without power, giving the pilot time to look for a clear space to land. But the aircraft were also flimsy. Sometimes a wing simply fell off in flight, and that was usually fatal.

Flying was uncomfortable, too. Cockpits were open to the elements. Pilots froze in cold weather and got soaked when it rained. In many aircraft the engine would spray the pilot with stinking castor oil.

Sticks and string

All early aircraft were made of wood, cloth, and piano wire, and were built by hand in small workshops. They also all had petrol engines and propellers. But in other ways they varied

wildly as inventive designers experimented with different approaches. Some flying machines had the propeller at the back, others at the front. Some, known as monoplanes, had one wing while others had two (biplanes) or even three (triplanes). Some back-to-front, so-called "canard" designs had the "tail" in front of the pilot. Many looked as though they shouldn't fly at all – and some of them didn't.

Two are better than one

Gradually, biplanes with a propeller at the front became the norm. Monoplanes were faster because they had fewer of the struts and wires that created so much drag. But the two wings of a biplane gave double the lift. Even more

THE BALCONY ON THE NOSE OF THE *ILYA MUROMETS* MULTI-ENGINED AIRCRAFT GAVE A GREAT, IF WINDY, VIEW.

importantly, biplanes could be made safer. Monoplanes tended to fall apart if the pilot turned too tightly!

Faster, higher…
The progress made in the first 10 years of the age of flight could be measured in speed. In 1903 the Wright *Flyer* had travelled at 48 kmh (30 mph), but by 1914 the world speed record was 147 kmh (92 mph).

By then, pilots had flown up to 6,100 m (20,000 ft) above the ground. They had also learned to perform breathtaking stunts such as looping-the-loop. And there were now aircraft fitted with floats that took off and landed on lakes or oceans.

And larger
Designers were also building larger planes. In 1913, a young Russian, Igor Sikorsky, designed the first aircraft with more than one engine. His *Ilya Muromets*, which flew the

A PASSENGER HOLDS ON TIGHT, READY TO FLY PERCHED ON THE WING OF A BIPLANE.

WEIRD WORLD
THE FIRST PARACHUTE JUMP FROM AN AIRPLANE WAS MADE IIN 1912. BUT THE BRITISH ARMY REFUSED TO GIVE ITS AIRMEN PARACHUTES, CLAIMING THAT IT WOULD ENCOURAGE COWARDICE.

following year, had four engines and could carry 16 people. It was the first aircraft with a lavatory and electric lights. It also had an open balcony in the nose where you could stand to get a magnificent view.

From fun to fighting
Despite these advances, aircraft remained mostly fun. They were expensive, grown-up toys for sport and recreation. This all changed in 1914, when World War I broke out in Europe. During the four years that the fighting lasted, tens of thousands of aircraft were built to fight the war in the air. Many people would look back with regret to the innocent times before flying machines became killing machines.

21

THE GOLDEN AGE

The 1920s and 1930s are often called the "golden age of flight." This was a time when fliers were worshipped as cool, glamorous, death-defying heroes, and could become as famous as monarchs or movie stars. Keeping them in the air were the latest aircraft designs, which flew ever further, higher, and faster, and gradually made flying a safer, more comfortable way to travel.

LINDBERGH INSPECTS THE ENGINE ON WHICH HIS LIFE DEPENDED BEFORE HIS ATLANTIC FLIGHT.

Daring dash

The most famous flier of the "golden age" was Charles Lindbergh, but on 20 May 1927 he was still just another unknown American pilot. That day he set off from New York in the hope of becoming the first person to fly non-stop to Paris.

Lindbergh nearly crashed on takeoff because his aircraft was so heavy, brim-full with petrol for the long flight. Once in the air he was totally alone. He had no radio. Just about all he had in his cramped cockpit was a clock, an unreliable compass, a water bottle, and five sandwiches. His ears were stuffed with cotton wool to keep out the deafening noise of the engine, and his view to the front was blocked by a large fuel tank. But he had a quiet determination to succeed.

S lim chance

People thought Lindbergh was crazy to try the 5,796-km (3,600-mile) flight solo and in a plane with only one engine.

Lindbergh was out of sight of land, with no hope of rescue if his engine failed and forced him to land in the hostile ocean. Through the night Lindbergh fought desperately to stay awake – if he fell asleep his aircraft would dive out of control. At moments he flew down dangerously close to the waves so that the icy spray on his face would keep him alert.

LINDBERGH'S AIRCRAFT WAS NAMED AFTER HIS SPONSORS – A GROUP OF BUSINESSMEN IN ST LOUIS, MISSOURI.

LINDBERGH YELLED DOWN TO A SHIP: "WHICH WAY IS IRELAND?"

Just the week before, two skilled French fliers, Francois Coli and Charles Nungesser, had disappeared on the way from Paris to New York. What chance did Lindbergh have?

The most dangerous part of the flight was crossing the Atlantic Ocean. For 15 hours

IN MAY 1932 FAMOUS AMERICAN FLIER AMELIA EARHART BECAME THE FIRST WOMAN TO FLY SOLO ACROSS THE ATLANTIC.

Lucky Lindy

Amazingly, Lindbergh not only stayed awake, but found his way across the featureless ocean. And his engine didn't let him down. When he landed in Paris, almost 34 hours after taking off, he was greeted with one of the wildest reception parties ever seen. The French called him "Lucky Lindy", though skill and sheer courage had been just as important.

Death or glory

Although no one could quite match Lindbergh's fame, plenty of other adventurers were prepared to risk their lives for fame and fortune. Every country had its heroes. The British celebrated John Alcock and Arthur Brown, who made the first non-stop flight across the Atlantic in 1919 – they landed nose down in an Irish bog. There were female flying stars too, none more famous than

America's Amelia Earhart, who became the first woman to fly solo across the Atlantic in 1932. Perhaps the strangest of the celebrities was Douglas Corrigan, who set out to fly from New York to California

A STUNT FLIER BALANCED ABOVE A COCKPIT PREPARES TO CLIMB FROM ONE AIRCRAFT TO ANOTHER IN MID-AIR. THESE STUNTS WERE EXTREMELY DANGEROUS.

in 1938, but got lost soon after take off and instead landed in Ireland. "Wrong Way Corrigan" was the toast of America!

Barnstorming

What made flying so exciting was the risk. In the United States, many pilots made a living as touring "barnstormers". They would put on incredible flying shows full of crazy stunts. A pilot might climb

BARNSTORMERS WENT TO EXTRAORDINARY
LENGTHS TO FIND NOVEL ACTS TO AMUSE
THE PUBLIC. TENNIS, ANYONE?

out of the cockpit while flying high above the ground and do handstands on the wing, or climb from one aircraft to another and back again in flight. To excite the crowds, barnstormers staged crashes, deliberately flying into buildings, or pretended to fall out of their aircraft by accident, not pulling their parachute ripcord until the very last moment. Some barnstormers gained national fame, like African American Bessie Coleman, who was affectionately known as "Queen Bess". They accepted danger in a devil-may-care spirit – one flier quipped that they were so badly paid, the worst risk was dying of starvation!

Racing demons

The US National Air Races excited massive interest. Some weird and wonderful people took part, such as pilot Roscoe Turner, who flew with a pet lion cub in his cockpit (it had its own parachute).

There were some outlandish aircraft too, designed for speed and nothing else. The Gee Bee Racer, for instance, was just a huge engine with stubby wings attached. It was incredibly hard to fly – five airmen were killed trying to master it. But ace pilot Jimmy Doolittle flew one to

WEIRD WORLD

ONE 1920S BARNSTORMING
GROUP LISTED FEES FOR
STUNTS: $250 TO STAGE A
BOXING BOUT ON A
WING; $1200 TO HIT
A HOUSE; $1500 TO
BLOW UP A PLANE IN
MID-AIR.

victory at the National Air Races in 1932 at an average speed of 476 kmh (296 mph).

S uper-fast seaplanes

At the time, though, the fastest aircraft in the world were seaplanes. Few airstrips had yet been built on land, and in any case the water provided a limitless runway. At the annual Schneider Trophy seaplane race in 1931, a Supermarine

F lying all over the world

But flight was not just for kicks. Fliers trailblazed routes that would one day be used for regular passenger flights. They flew over deserts and great mountain ranges, down the length of Africa, and across the wastes

IN 1932 AN ENGLAND-AUSTRALIA FLIGHT TOOK OVER EIGHT DAYS

became the first aircraft to fly at over 644 kmh (400 mph) – faster than any human had ever travelled before.

of central Asia, bringing contact with the outside world to places without roads, railways, or telephones.

The fliers were not always welcome. When famous French pilot Jean Mermoz was forced to crash-land in the Sahara Desert, he was captured by tribesmen, who only let him go after a ransom was paid.

SUPERMARINE

WINNER OF THE 1922
INTERNATIONAL 1927
SCHNEIDER
1929
TROPHY

Supermarine Rolls-Royce S.6

HOLDER OF THE
WORLD'S
SPEED
RECORD
357·7 M.P.H.

DESIGNED AND CONSTRUCTED TO THE
ORDER OF THE BRITISH AIR MINISTRY

THE SUPERMARINE AVIATION WORKS
(VICKERS) LIMITED
SOUTHAMPTON, ENGLAND.
LONDON OFFICE: VICKERS HOUSE, BROADWAY, WESTMINSTER, S.W.1.

SUPERMARINE PUBLICIZES THE SUCCESS OF ITS RACING SEAPLANES. REGINALD MITCHELL, WHO DESIGNED PLANES FOR THE COMPANY, LATER CREATED THE SPITFIRE FIGHTER.

THE GEE BEE WAS ONE OF THE FASTEST PLANES OF THE 1930S. HERE A PILOT FLIES HIS RESTORED PLANE "INVERTED" OVER THE SOUTHWESTERN UNITED STATES.

Pioneers in peril

Every pilot who took part in extending flight across the world had their close shaves. Many lost their lives, especially flying over the empty oceans. Australia's most famous flier, Charles Kingsford Smith, disappeared in the Indian Ocean while flying from England to Australia in 1935. Jean Mermoz disappeared over the South Atlantic Ocean in 1936. Amelia Earhart vanished in the Pacific while attempting a round-the-world flight in 1937. Hundreds of fliers suffered similar fates, but they proved that long-distance flight was a reality.

Air rescue

But aircraft were mostly seen as a great advance. If you lived on a remote farm in the Australian outback during the 1920s, it was a great relief when the first "flying doctor" service started. At last, you could call for urgent medical care that might arrive in time to save a life. In many parts of the globe, air mail brought regular delivery of letters for the first time – another lifeline to the outside world.

IN THE 1930S, HUGE WIND-TUNNELS
WERE BUILT TO TEST NEW
AIRCRAFT DESIGNS.

What a drag

It was German planemaker Hugo Junkers who showed how to make monoplanes with metal wings that did not need struts or wires to hold them firm. The new, streamlined aircraft slipped through the air with less drag (resistance).

Designers

The pilots could not have done what they did without the efforts of aircraft designers and engineers, who made aeroplanes that flew faster and further than ever before.

Partly this was through better engines, which just kept getting more powerful, as well as much more reliable. A 1930s aircraft engine might generate 10 or 20 times more power than in the days of Louis Blériot.

There was also a great leap forward in the way aircraft were designed. Clumsy contraptions of canvas, wood, and wire were on the way out. In their place were sleek new machines of smooth, shiny aluminium and steel.

In the wind

Engineers using giant wind-tunnels found other ways to reduce drag. They proved, for instance, that having the wheels sticking out all the time in flight added unwanted drag.

So aircraft were built with retractable undercarriages – the wheels pulled up into the fuselage or wing after take off and were lowered again for landing. This made an enormous improvement to an aeroplane's performance.

Flying on auto

With better aircraft came better instruments to help pilots fly them. Until the 1930s, most airmen flew "by the seat of their pants", trusting more to their instincts than to the dials in their cockpit which were as likely to be wrong as right.

But even experienced pilots admitted that flying at night or in heavy cloud was safer when you had radio, a compass that really worked, and an "artificial horizon" dial to show you which way up you were. When one-eyed American airman Wiley Post flew solo around the world in 1933 he had an automatic pilot in his aircraft, which held the plane steady and level while he took a nap.

End of an era

By the end of the 1930s the golden age of air heroes was drawing to an end, because better aircraft and instruments were beginning to make flying reasonably safe. That's why, today, no one needs the courage and blind luck of a Lindbergh to cross the Atlantic – just a passport and a ticket.

LOG ON...
www.geocities.com/Cape
Canaveral/Lab/4515/history.html

THE GERMAN FIRM JUNKERS WAS THE FIRST TO MAKE ALL-METAL AIRCRAFT, LIKE THIS THREE-ENGINED 1930S AIRLINER.

LUFTHANSA
BERLIN-TEMPELHOF

SHIPS OF THE AIR

About four times the size of a jumbo jet, the *Hindenburg* was the largest aircraft ever to fly. It was the most celebrated of the airships, which offered rich passengers a luxurious cruise in an era when planes were widely seen as dangerous toys. If airships had not turned out to be even more unsafe, the future of air travel might well have been cigar-shaped.

Lap of luxury

The *Hindenburg* was more like a ship than a plane. It was steered by a man standing at a nautical wheel, while dozens of crew warmed along gangways inside its silver-grey skin.

In the 1930s, the *Hindenburg* carried passengers from Europe to North America. The trip took two to three days, but what it lacked in speed, it made up for in style. Next time you sit in an airline seat, eating a meal off a tray, picture yourself as a passenger on the *Hindenburg*.

You could stroll on the promenade deck and peer down through

MAIDS PREPARE TO SERVE TEA IN THE LUXURIOUS DINING ROOM OF THE BRITISH AIRSHIP *R100*.

slopimg windows to the ocean.
The distant engine hum was
broken only by the sounding of
a gong calling you to dinner.
You would use
the finest white
linen and silver
cutlery, while
waiters served you a
gourmet meal and a
pianist tinkled away
at a piano. When you

than-air gas that kept the
airship aloft. But hydrogen is
highly flammable. All it needed
was a stray spark and a slight
gas leak – and
then *whoomph*!
The gasbags of
the *Hindenburg*
were made from a
material known as
goldbeater's skin,
used because it did

felt tired, you could retire to
bed in your own cosy cabin, or
freshen up under a hot shower.

Deadly gasbags

But there was a downside to all
this. Most of the *Hindenburg*'s
bulk consisted of huge bags
filled with hydrogen, a lighter-

THE GERMAN AIRSHIP *HINDENBURG* BORE
THE SWASTIKA, SYMBOL OF THE NAZI
REGIME THAT THEN RULED GERMANY.

not create sparks. Goldbeater's
skin may sound fancy, but it's
actually just the lining of a
cow's stomach. It took a million
stomach linings to make the
gasbags for a single airship!

AN AIRSHIP BEING BUILT SHOWS THE
LIGHTWEIGHT ALUMINIUM-ALLOY FRAME
USUALLY HIDDEN BY ITS OUTER ENVELOPE.

LOG ON...
www.history1900s.about.com
/library/weekly/aa102600a.htm

Not even a million cows could make hydrogen safe to use. Helium would have been a much safer gas; it was lighter than air, and it didn't burn. But the only source of helium in the world was in Texas, and the United States wouldn't share it. Everyone else had to put up with hydrogen gas.

E arly risers

Despite the safety problem, airships had long held the lead over aeroplanes. The first powered flight was made not by the Wrights, but by Henri Giffard, a Frenchman. In 1852 he fitted a small steam engine to a balloon and

steered his "dirigible" around the sky.

In 1901, Brazilian-born Parisian Alberto Santos-Dumont flew an airship for half an hour around the Eiffel Tower – and this was at a time when the Wright brothers were still testing gliders.

Z eppelin

The man whose name is forever associated with airships was Count Zeppelin, a German aristocrat. He built his first airship in 1900, and by 1910 had developed his "zeppelins" until they were reliable enough to carry sightseers on trips.

In World War I, zeppelins found a more sinister use. Chugging through the night skies across the North Sea, German airships dropped bombs on London and other parts of England. They caused a great deal of fear but not much damage, and many were shot down in flames.

HENRI GIFFARD'S STEAM-
POWERED DIRIGIBLE FLEW AT
ABOUT 8 KMH (5 MPH) IN STILL
AIR – IT COULDN'T MAKE ANY
HEADWAY INTO THE WIND.

A ircraft carriers

After World War I, the United States Navy became interested in airships, which they wanted

33

to use as airborne aircraft carriers. This idea was not quite as daft as it might sound.

The Navy would hook half a dozen small fighter aircraft onto the underside of an airship. When it was time for a mission, a pilot climbed into one of the fighters and the hook was released to launch it. When the fighter returned it hooked onto the airship again in flight – this was a tricky manoeuvre, but not impossible.

Unfit for duty

The reason the "airborne aircraft carrier" idea didn't work was because, even with helium instead of hydrogen, the US Navy couldn't make its airships safe. In a howling gale or a storm, airships were bad places to be. They just kept on crashing. Eventually, the Americans gave up on them.

Britain had a catastrophic experience with airships. In October 1930, a new British airship, *R101*, set off on its maiden flight from England to India with a lot of VIPs

on board for the special occasion. It got no further than France. On a night of wind and rain it crashed into a hillside, killing 48 of the 54 on board.

German confidence

Only the Germans seemed to be able to fly airships successfully. In 1929 the *Graf Zeppelin* carried 53 passengers and crew on a three-week journey right around the world. Joined by the even bigger *Hindenburg*, it established regular and reliable – though immensely expensive – services across the Atlantic.

The Germans believed that the future of air travel was gas-filled, and some Americans agreed with them. New York's Empire State Building was built with a docking mast for airships at its tip. But their optimism was soon to be crushed.

A 46-M (150-FT) MOORING MAST FOR AIRSHIPS ONCE FORMED THE TOP OF NEW YORK'S EMPIRE STATE BUILDING.

Disaster!

The zeppelin's future ended suddenly on the evening of 6 May 1937. The *Hindenburg* had arrived at Lakehurst, New Jersey, after a regular run from Europe. As it docked, a lick of flame appeared at the stern. The probable cause was a spark

THE *HINDENBURG* BURNS IN 1937. SPARKS OF STATIC ELECTRICITY ON THE FLAMMABLE SKIN MAY HAVE STARTED THE FIRE.

of static electricity igniting the paint on the skin. The gas then caught fire, resulting in an inferno. Amazingly, 62 of the 97 people on board survived. Even more might have lived had they waited for the airship to sink a little. Instead, many leaped off at once in panic.

The *Hindenburg* disaster was the end of airship travel. Linked in people's imaginations with the idea of a fiery death, airships became extinct, like dinosaurs of the skies.

WEIRD WORLD

OUT OF 161 AIRSHIPS BUILT, 60 WERE DESTROYED IN ACCIDENTS. IF MODERN AIRLINERS WERE THAT ACCIDENT-PRONE, IT'S ESTIMATED THAT THERE WOULD NOW BE 12 MAJOR AIR CRASHES EVERY DAY!

TRAVELLING IN STYLE

In the early days of air travel, flying was a genuine adventure for the few passengers who tried it. They needed strong nerves and a strong stomach, as well as a healthy bank balance. But if there was discomfort, there was style and luxury as well, until progress in aircraft design and air traffic control made air travel what it is today – safe, easy, but also a little less fun.

PASSENGERS BOARD A FORD TRIMOTOR, THE "TIN GOOSE" THAT WAS AMERICA'S TOP AIRLINER IN THE 1920S.

Hot and bothered

It's the 1920s and you're crossing the United States in a Ford "Tin Goose", the very latest in airliner design.

A dozen passengers are sitting on two rows of wicker chairs. It's a hot day and they're sweating in the small passenger cabin – if it was winter they'd be shivering in overcoats.

Fortunately, they can open the windows for some fresh air – but this also lets in the full roar of the three engines.

However, even with the windows shut the engine noise is deafening, like sitting next to a pneumatic drill – which is why you're given earplugs when you board.

You must remember not to throw things out of the windows, especially over towns. People on the ground need to watch out, too, particularly since

PASSENGERS HAD TO BE WEIGHED AS WELL AS THEIR LUGGAGE, TO MAKE SURE THE PLANE WASN'T OVERLOADED.

PASSENGERS ON A SCENIC FLIGHT OVER LAKE GENEVA IN 1929 KEEP THEIR COATS ON IN THE DRAUGHTY AEROPLANE.

everything that goes into the lavatory falls straight out through a hole in the bottom of the fuselage!

Sick and shaken

The flight is much worse in bad weather. Then the plane bumps around like a fairground ride. Passengers are soon filling their "burp cups" with vomit – and this can go on for hours. (The first air stewardesses employed in 1930 were qualified nurses to look after airsick passengers.)

If the weather gets too bad, the pilot makes an emergency landing at a small airstrip or even on a farm field, and the shaken passengers finish their trip by train, probably relieved to be back on the ground.

Where are we?

Regular passenger services by aeroplane had started in Europe in 1919. But as you've seen, early air travel was not comfortable – and it wasn't that safe, either. In the 1920s, pilots still mostly followed roads or railways to find their way, especially in low cloud or

AIR TRAFFIC CONTROL 1920S STYLE: AN OFFICIAL WAVES A RED FLAG TO TELL AN AIRLINE PILOT THAT THE RUNWAY IS NOT YET CLEAR.

37

fog. Cutting across country was a recipe for getting utterly lost. And if two pilots were following the same road or railway in opposite directions – ouch! The only form of air traffic control was at airfields, cleared them to take off or land. And so that aircraft could travel safely by night, lines of giant beacons were set up along major airways, like lighthouses shining powerful beams high into the sky.

PASSENGERS SOMETIMES HAD TO LEAN OVER TO HELP PLANES TURN

where a man waved a green flag to show it was safe to land and a red flag if it wasn't.

Lighting the way

Of course, things had to improve. By the 1930s, in Europe and the United States, proper airports were being built and "airways" were marked out – routes for airliners to follow from city to city. Once airliners were fitted with radios they could talk to controllers at airports, who

Smoothing out the bumps

New aircraft made journeys quicker and more comfortable. The Douglas DC-3, launched in 1936, carried 21 passengers across the United States from coast to coast in about 18 hours, operating overnight and in most weather conditions. Reasonable sound-proofing and shock absorbers made the seating less

Islander

bone-shaking. There were in-
flight meals much like we have
today, but no entertainment.
Though not appealing enough
to tempt most people away
from rail travel, it was a start.

B y air and water

If you wanted to fly across
oceans or to remote lands in
the 1930s, you went by flying
boat. These beautiful machines
had wings attached to what was
basically a boat hull. When
they landed on water they hit
with a thump, and spray
splashed the windows. But
people on ocean journeys felt
safer in an aircraft that
could land on the sea.

Flying boats opened up new
routes, from England to South
Africa for example, and from
California to Hong Kong.
These journeys could take from
a few days to more than a

BECAUSE OF THEIR
LARGE HULLS, FLYING
BOATS LIKE THIS
SHORT SUNDERLAND
WERE MUCH MORE
SPACIOUS INSIDE
THAN AIRLINERS
THAT OPERATED
FROM LAND.

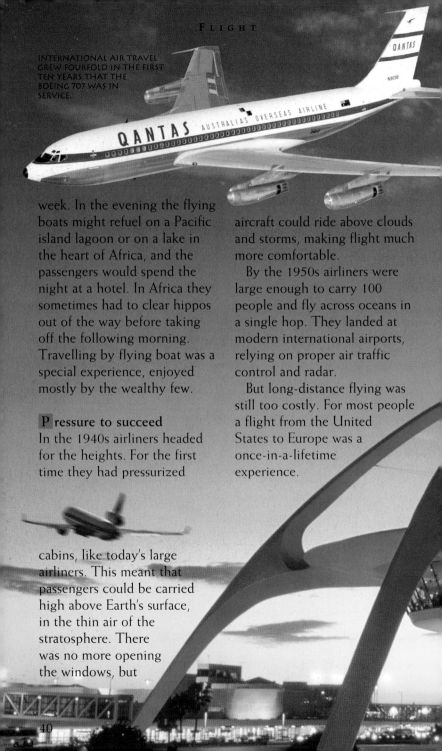

INTERNATIONAL AIR TRAVEL GREW FOURFOLD IN THE FIRST TEN YEARS THAT THE BOEING 707 WAS IN SERVICE.

week. In the evening the flying boats might refuel on a Pacific island lagoon or on a lake in the heart of Africa, and the passengers would spend the night at a hotel. In Africa they sometimes had to clear hippos out of the way before taking off the following morning. Travelling by flying boat was a special experience, enjoyed mostly by the wealthy few.

Pressure to succeed

In the 1940s airliners headed for the heights. For the first time they had pressurized cabins, like today's large airliners. This meant that passengers could be carried high above Earth's surface, in the thin air of the stratosphere. There was no more opening the windows, but aircraft could ride above clouds and storms, making flight much more comfortable.

By the 1950s airliners were large enough to carry 100 people and fly across oceans in a single hop. They landed at modern international airports, relying on proper air traffic control and radar.

But long-distance flying was still too costly. For most people a flight from the United States to Europe was a once-in-a-lifetime experience.

The age of jet travel

When jet airliners arrived, long-distance travel really took off. The jet-powered Boeing 707, which began flights across the Atlantic in 1958, travelled at up to 960 kmh (600 mph), twice as fast as propeller airliners. It halved the time it took to fly from New York to London or Paris – and reduced the journey's cost, too.

Mass transportation

Now that flying was easy and relatively inexpensive, it was within the reach of people who had never before dreamed of taking to the air. By the start of the 21st century, jet airliners worldwide were carrying more than a billion passengers a year. No one thought it odd to hop on a plane for a holiday in New York or New Zealand. No two cities on the planet were more than 24 hours apart.

Juan Trippe, the boss of PanAm, the first airline to use the Boeing 707, described the new era neatly: "We have shrunken the earth."

THE FUTURISTIC LOOK OF LOS ANGELES AIRPORT SUMS UP THE DISTANCE AIR TRAVEL HAS COME SINCE THE ERA OF THE "TIN GOOSE" AND THE RED WARNING FLAG.

WEIRD WORLD

IN 2001 CHICAGO O'HARE, THE WORLD'S BUSIEST AIRPORT, HANDLED 912,000 FLIGHTS – AROUND 2,500 A DAY. MORE THAN A MILLION PEOPLE PASS THROUGH O'HARE EACH WEEK.

WINGS FOR VICTORY

It is sad but true that one of the major uses of aircraft has always been for war. Early airplanes were so unreliable and difficult to fly that they were more likely to kill their pilots than anyone else. But over time warplanes became fearsomely powerful machines, armed with an array of bombs, missiles, and guns. The fighter pilots of two World Wars were popular heroes.

IN 1914, THE TECHNIQUE OF DROPPING BOMBS WAS PRIMITIVE. EVEN FLYING AT LOW LEVEL, YOU WERE UNLIKELY TO HIT A PRECISE TARGET.

Don't frighten the horses

When aircraft were first invented, wars were still fought by men on horseback or on foot. Some old-fashioned army officers wanted nothing to do with the newfangled flying machines – they were afraid that the noise of the engines might frighten their horses.

But it was obvious that even the primitive aircraft of those days might be of use in warfare. Moving fast and flying high, they could act as "eyes in the sky", reporting back on enemy movements. And they might be able to drop things on the enemy – bombs, for example.

IN 1918 MORE AMERICAN PILOTS DIED TRAINING THAN FIGHTING

So, on the whole, military men welcomed the new invention, even if they weren't sure how helpful it would be.

42

The first warplanes

In 1914, the whole of Europe was engulfed in World War I. Millions of soldiers went off to battle, and so did a few hundred flimsy aircraft. While the soldiers dug into trenches, the aircraft flew overhead, taking

To guard its forces, each side sent up planes to shoot down the enemy. At first airmen fired at one another with pistols or rifles, but it was not long before aeroplanes went up equipped

LOG ON...
For World War I aces, visit www.theaerodrome.com

A WORLD WAR I "DOGFIGHT" IS STAGED BETWEEN AN ALLIED S.E.5A BIPLANE AND THE FAMOUS RED FOKKER TRIPLANE FLOWN BY GERMAN ACE BARON MANFRED VON RICHTHOFEN.

with machine-guns. They were the first fighter aircraft.

photographs of their positions. Sometimes they might drop a bomb by hand over the side of the plane.

Dogfights

Fighters spent most of their time shooting down almost defenceless reconnaissance or

43

bomber aircraft. But sometimes they engaged in "dogfights", air battles in which dozens of fighter aircraft dodged and dived, trying to get an enemy in their sights without being shot down themselves.

Journalists hailed the fighter pilots as "knights of the air". The top pilots, called "aces", became legendary heroes.

The Red Baron

None was more famous than the German Baron Manfred von Richthofen. Known as the Red Baron, he was credited with 80 "kills". Richthofen's fighter squadron was nicknamed "Richthofen's Flying Circus", because all the aircraft were painted in different bright colours. But like many other aces, Richthofen was killed in action before the war was over.

The bombing menace

By the time World War I ended in 1918, it had involved tens of thousands of aircraft.

In a frightening development, aeroplanes and airships had bombed towns and cities. Only relatively small numbers of people were killed, because the aircraft were not powerful enough to carry many bombs over a long distance. But these air raids were terrifying for ordinary people. They knew that, if there was ever another major war, aircraft would play an even bigger role, and bombing of cities was likely to happen on a terrifying scale.

WEIRD WORLD

REGINALD MITCHELL, THE SPITFIRE'S DESIGNER, HATED THE PLANE'S "SILLY NAME". IT COULD HAVE BEEN WORSE – THE SAME FIRM CALLED ANOTHER PLANE THE SHREW!

AT THE TIME OF THE BATTLE OF BRITAIN, IN THE SUMMER OF 1940, THE SPITFIRE WAS THE ONLY BRITISH FIGHTER THAT COULD MATCH THE PERFORMANCE OF THE BEST GERMAN AIRCRAFT.

Terror from the skies

During the 1930s, Nazi Germany's Luftwaffe became the most feared air force in the world. Luftwaffe is a German word meaning "air weapon", and its deadly power was revealed when pilots and aircraft were sent to join in a civil war that raged in Spain.

In 1937, Luftwaffe dive-bombers attacked the small town of Guernica in Spain's Basque region. Many people were killed and half the town was blown up.

THE MESSERSCHMITT BF 109 WAS THE SPITFIRE'S ARCH-ENEMY IN THE AIR DUELS OF THE BATTLE OF BRITAIN.

Air battle

When World War II broke out in 1939, bringing Britain and France into conflict with Nazi Germany, millions of British children were evacuated from cities to the countryside for fear of bombing.

In the summer of 1940 the Battle of Britain was fought, the first battle to take place exclusively in the air. The Luftwaffe tried to destroy Britain's Royal Air Force (RAF) by bombing its airfields. Fighters escorted the slow bombers in order to protect them from RAF fighters.

Luckily for the RAF, it had a new invention – radar – to detect incoming aircraft. This gave the RAF early warning of air raids, enabling it to "scramble" its fighters into the air to meet the intruders.

RAF Spitfires and Hurricanes took on Messerschmitt fighters and their fleets of bombers in the skies over southern England. Usually outnumbered, the RAF kept on fighting until the Luftwaffe had to accept it couldn't win control of the air. British prime minister Winston Churchill celebrated the RAF's

A LUFTWAFFE BOMBER CREW IN THEIR CRAMPED COCKPIT PREPARE TO RELEASE THEIR BOMBS OVER BRITAIN DURING A NIGHT RAID.

pilots in a famous phrase: "Never had so much been owed by so many to so few."

Cities under fire

The Germans then turned to attacking British cities by night. This was called the "Blitz".

Whenever the bombers came over, a warning sounded and people took cover in air raid shelters. Londoners slept on Underground station platforms to avoid the bombs.

The German raids caused great damage and killed many thousands of people. But German cities eventually suffered far more heavily.

Allies strike back

Like the Luftwaffe, the RAF bombed by night. At first, lost in the dark, its bombers could rarely hit the right city, let alone a particular district. Then planes were fitted with radar and radio to navigate at night.

German defenders also used radar on their anti-aircraft guns and night fighters to find the raiders, so that battles were fought between enemies who saw one another only as blips on a screen.

RAF night raids grew to vast proportions, often with up to a thousand four-engined bombers dropping millions of pounds of explosives on their targets in a single operation.

AMERICA'S B-17 BOMBER WAS CALLED THE "FLYING FORTRESS" BECAUSE IT WAS DEFENDED BY THE FIREPOWER OF 13 MACHINE GUNS.

America enters the fray

After the United States entered the war in 1941, its aircraft bombed Germany in daylight.

FACTORIES MASS-PRODUCED AIRCRAFT ON A HUGE SCALE IN WORLD WAR II. MORE THAN 12,000 OF THESE B-17S WERE BUILT.

Boeing B-17 Flying Fortresses and B-24 Liberators bristled with guns for protection against the Luftwaffe fighters.

Operating mostly from air bases in eastern England, the American planes had a crew of up to 10 men. On the B-17 one gunner sat in a ball turret, hanging under the aircraft's belly. The bombers flew at high altitude, their crew wearing oxygen masks and heated suits to stave off the cold. Attacking in swarms of hundreds, they scored many more direct hits than the RAF. German air

THE FEARSOME JAWS ON THIS CURTISS FIGHTER WERE THE SYMBOL OF THE "FLYING TIGERS", A GROUP OF US PILOTS WHO FOUGHT THE JAPANESE IN BURMA AND CHINA.

defences were strong, and thousands of bombers were shot down, but Germany suffered enormous damage and loss of life.

Carriers
Meanwhile, the war at sea had also become an air war. Navies were traditionally proud of their battleships – big armoured vessels with powerful guns. The idea that an aircraft could sink one of these warships had once been thought ridiculous.

This was proved wrong by American air commander Billy Mitchell in 1921. He staged a

47

demonstration in which his Martin biplane bombers sank a captured German battleship, the supposedly "unsinkable" *Ostfriesland*, in a mere 21 minutes. This encouraged navies to add aircraft carriers to their fleets, though battleships were still seen as the main war-winners at sea.

Pearl Harbor

The US Navy changed its mind after 7 December 1941. On that day the Japanese launched a surprise attack on the American naval base at Pearl Harbor in Hawaii. Japanese bombers and torpedo aircraft, launched from aircraft carriers, sank a large part of the US Pacific fleet in a few hours, including five battleships. More than 2,400 personnel died.

destroyed the Japanese carriers, while US fighters shot down the Japanese planes.

Kamikaze!

In the last year of the war, the Japanese adopted a desperate new tactic: suicide attacks. So-called kamikaze pilots flew their Mitsubishi "Zero" and Aichi "Val" aircraft straight at US warships, aiming at points where their exploding bombs and fuel would cause the most damage, such as the aircraft hangars of carriers. They were also taught words to shout at the last

EACH B-1 BOMBER COST ABOUT US$200 MILLION TO BUILD

The Pacific War between the United States and Japan turned into a contest between aircraft carriers. American carrier-launched torpedo aircraft and dive-bombers eventually

moment in order to bolster their courage. Though this tactic used up many pilots and aircraft, it also sank several ships. It could not, however, prevent Japan's defeat.

AMERICA'S B-1B LANCER, BUILT IN THE 1980S, IS A SUPERSONIC BOMBER THAT LOOKS AND PERFORMS LIKE A FIGHTER.

Aircraft everywhere

By the end of World War II aircraft had been produced in their hundreds of thousands and were serving on every battle front. They flew over deserts, jungles and mountains. From air transports, such as the German Junkers Ju-52, thousands of troops parachuted behind enemy lines or near key objectives. Ground-attack planes, such as the Republic P-47 Thunderbolt or Hawker Typhoon, destroyed tanks and trucks.

Warplanes today

Since the war, military aircraft have got faster, with longer range and more powerful and highly accurate weaponry. Their role in war has, if anything, increased. But they have never again played a decisive part in quite such an important victory.

49

FASTER THAN SOUND

At the dawn of the "jet age" in the late 1940s, the skies echoed with the roars and screams of experimental planes. Powered by jets or rockets, their target was to travel faster than sound itself. However, test pilots found out the hard way that aeroplanes behave in very strange ways as they approach the speed of sound. For a while it seemed that the goal of "going supersonic" was to remain an impossible dream – a sound barrier.

Test tragedy

In September 1946, test pilot Geoffrey de Havilland took an experimental jet aircraft, the D.H. 108, into the air over England. He intended to fly it faster than any plane had gone before – faster than sound. He put the aircraft into a dive to gain speed. But as he neared the speed of sound, a violent shaking battered the aeroplane, as if it were a car being driven very fast over a rocky road.

Suddenly and terrifyingly, the flight controls stopped operating. However hard de Havilland pulled on the control stick, it made no difference. Accelerating out of control, the D.H. 108 broke up in the air.

Shocking speed

De Havilland was killed, but we know what he must have experienced that day because something like it happened to

AN F/A-18 HORNET IS SHOWN AS IT BREAKS THE SOUND BARRIER. THE STRANGE CLOUD IS WATER CONDENSATION CAUSED BY THE SHOCK WAVE THE AEROPLANE CREATES AS IT SPEEDS THROUGH THE AIR.

other pilots who lived to tell the tale. The actual speed of sound in miles or kilometres per hour varies, but it is always referred to as Mach 1. When an aircraft accelerates towards

Mach 1, it runs into shock waves created by its own passage through the air.

To fliers of de Havilland's generation it seemed as if it might be impossible to fly through this "sound barrier".

THIS D.H. 108 WAS THE PLANE IN WHICH TEST PILOT GEOFFREY DE HAVILLAND DIED WHILE TRYING TO GO SUPERSONIC IN 1946.

Propellers meet their limit

This was a big issue in the 1940s because new jet and rocket engines had been invented that were clearly going to make aircraft much, much faster. Until then all aircraft had been powered by propellers turned by piston engines (essentially like the engine of a car, but larger).

A very fast piston-engined aircraft, such as the World War II Mustang fighter, could reach about 720 kmh (450 mph) in level flight. This was as good as you were going to get out of a piston engine and prop.

Jets and rockets

Jet and rockets are completely different. Anyone who has made a party balloon whiz around a room knows the basic principle – air rushing out of a hole at the back thrusts the balloon forwards. Powering an aircraft this way, there was virtually no limit to the top speed – if only the sound barrier could be overcome.

How engines work

In a rocket engine, a stream of hot air is created by burning chemicals, just like when you light a firework. As long as the chemical goes on burning, the rocket zips across the sky. Space rockets carry their own supply of liquid oxygen, so they can travel in the airless emptiness of outer space.

Jet engines are more useful for aircraft. They take in air at the front, heat and compress it, and then push it out of a hole at the back

WEIRD WORLD
THE LOUDEST SONIC BOOM EVER RECORDED CAME FROM A LOW-FLYING F-4 PHANTOM JET. THE SOUND WAS 70 TIMES AS STRONG AS THE BOOM TYPICALLY MADE BY A HIGH-FLYING CONCORDE.

51

(although it isn't always that simple). The important thing about jet engines is that they work better the faster you go and the higher you fly.

Germany's jets

The first jet aircraft engines were designed in the 1930s by Frank Whittle in Britain and Hans von Ohain in Germany.

The Nazis quickly pushed ahead with jets and rockets. During the later stages of did of the enemy. But they were definitely the fastest machines in the sky.

Guinea pigs

After the war, solving the mystery of the sound barrier became a major priority. Nowadays, it would probably be possible to use computer models to work out what was going on. But the only way to study it back in those days was to send a test pilot up in an aircraft and see what happened.

THE X-1 FLEW FOR JUST TWO AND A HALF MINUTES ON FULL POWER

World War II (1939–45) Messerschmitt Me163 rocket planes and Me262 jet fighters flew in the defence of Germany against Allied bombers. They were still experimental aircraft and scary to fly, killing almost as many of their pilots as they

The Americans built an experimental rocket plane, the Bell X-1, for the purpose, and found a test pilot, Chuck Yeager, ready to risk his life pushing it to the limit. Yeager called his Bell X-1 *Glamorous Glennis*, after his wife.

THE MESSERSCHMITT ME262 WAS THE FIRST JET FIGHTER. FLYING IN THE 1940S, IT HAD A TOP SPEED OF 870 KMH (541 MPH), MUCH FASTER THAN ANY PISTON-ENGINED PLANE OF ITS DAY.

LOG ON...
Read about Yeager at www.chuckyeager.com

What a ride!

For test flights, the rocket plane was carried up to high altitude underneath a Boeing B-29 bomber. That way, the X-1 didn't need fuel for take-off.

Yeager climbed down into the tiny cockpit, and the X-1 was dropped out of the B-29 like a bomb. Seconds later he ignited his rocket engine and accelerated into a few minutes of high-speed flight. "God what a ride!" he later wrote.

As the X-1 drew close to Mach 1, Yeager met the usual unnerving experiences of extreme turbulence and loss of control. But a change to the way the control surfaces worked overcame the initial control problem. The turbulence was no longer so violent as Yeager crept towards the very edge of the speed of sound.

THE BELL X-1 ROCKET PLANE IS DROPPED FROM THE BELLY OF THE B-29 "MOTHERSHIP" THAT TOOK IT TO HIGH ALTITUDE.

When the test was over, he switched off his engine and glided back down to land.

Yeager carried out a series of these flights, gradually upping the speed, while scientists on the ground monitored him.

On 14 October 1947, during his ninth X-1 flight, Yeager was in pain after falling from a horse at the weekend and breaking two ribs. Not wishing to be grounded, he kept the injury a secret. And although still forbidden by his cautious controllers to "go supersonic", he decided to go for it anyway.

People on the ground heard an ear-shattering boom. It was a noise never before heard on earth – the sonic boom that an aircraft delivers when it is flying faster than sound.

3,220 kmh (2,000 mph), but he did not live to enjoy his fame. He was killed as the X-2 flew out of control and crashed in the course of the record-breaking Mach 3 flight.

These experiments with rocket planes reached a climax with the X-15A-2. In 1967 it reached Mach 6.72 – twice the speed of a rifle bullet!

Yeager later wrote that after he passed Mach 1, "It was as smooth as a baby's bottom. Grandma could be sitting up there sipping

THE X-15, THE FASTEST WINGED AEROPLANE EVER, FIRED SMALL JETS TO TURN AT HIGH ALTITUDE – LIKE THE JETS THAT SPACECRAFT USE IN SPACE.

THE X-15 FLEW UP TO 108 KM (67 MILES) ABOVE THE EARTH

lemonade." The sound barrier was broken and the way was open to higher speeds.

Faster still

Rocket aircraft launched from bombers went on to break speed records again and again. In 1953 the Douglas Skyrocket passed Mach 2 (twice the speed of sound). In 1956 the Bell X-2 exceeded Mach 3. The X-2's pilot, Milburn Apt, was the first human to travel at over

Fast fighters

Jet aircraft that took off from the ground couldn't match the X-15's speed. That was only bettered by the Space Shuttle in 1981. Soon, however, jet fighters went supersonic. The F-104 Starfighter flew at Mach 2 in level flight, and even faster in a dive – they called it "the missile with a man in it"!

These amazing speeds carried terrible risks. Many test pilots and ordinary fighter pilots died young. Parachutes were useless in aircraft moving that fast, so ejection seats were brought in. But being blown out of your cockpit strapped in a seat was also extremely dangerous, even if it was better than ending up amid the twisted wreckage of your aircraft.

Today the maximum speed of jet fighter aircraft is not much faster than 40 years ago. For practical purposes, Mach 2 was fast enough. Instead, jet planes have improved in other ways, from electronic control systems to more reliable engines. This has taken most of the danger out of supersonic flight.

Yet, while today's fighter pilots are kitted out like astronauts, the only protection Yeager had on his flights was an American football helmet! The test pilots of the 1940s and 1950s were true heroes.

A MODERN JET FIGHTER PILOT SITS IN AN EJECTION SEAT. IN AN EMERGENCY, THE SEAT CAN FIRE THE PILOT FROM THE COCKPIT AT ABOUT 160 KMH (100 MPH).

HAPPY LANDINGS!

Take-off and landing have always been the trickiest moments in flight. It's hard enough setting a fully laden airliner down on a busy airport runway, but what if your airstrip is a rolling ship's deck or a forest clearing in a war zone? Progress in aircraft design and the use of electronic instruments have made getting up and down easier and, in some cases, quite spectacular.

Belt up

Flying is safer than driving, but as you fasten your seat-belt at the start of a flight it's hard not to feel a little nervous. This, after all, is one of the two riskiest

IN 1954 THE ROLLS-ROYCE "FLYING BEDSTEAD" TRIED OUT VERTICAL TAKE-OFF WITH JETS ON EACH OF ITS LEGS.

A FULL JUMBO JET NEEDS OVER 3,300 M (3,609 YD) OF RUNWAY

periods of the flight. Luckily, airlines know how to plot the safest way into the air.

As you sit at the start of the airport runway, the crew have already worked out what speed they will need to leave the ground. This depends on the weight of the plane with its load of passengers. The more weight there is, the more speed you need. It also depends on conditions at the airport – wind strength and direction, air temperature, and so on.

Another important factor is fuel. An aeroplane is heaviest at take-off, when it is fully fuelled.

56

A BOEING B-47 STRATOJET BOMBER OF THE
1950S BLASTS INTO THE AIR WITH THE
SPECTACULAR ASSISTANCE OF ROCKETS
UNDER ITS TAIL. ONCE IN FLIGHT, THE
PLANE FLEW SOLELY BY JET POWER.

The longer
the flight, the
more fuel is
needed, and so
the more difficult
it is to take off. On
the other hand, the
longer the runway, the
more chance there is of
working up enough speed
to get airborne.

As soon as the airliner is
cleared for take-off, the pilot
sets the engines to full power
and accelerates down the
runway. As the aircraft reaches
the take-off speed, the pilot
pulls back on the controls. This
brings the aircraft's nose up –
and away she goes!

Assisted take-off
The first people to have
problems finding enough
power to take off were
the Wright brothers.
The year after their
famous first flights
at Kitty Hawk,
they tried to fly
again near their home at
Dayton, Ohio – and they
couldn't get off the
ground! This was
because conditions
were warmer, at a
higher altitude, and
without a strong
headwind. So
they invented
a catapult to
propel their
Flyer to a

high enough speed to lift off the ground. This is now called an "assisted take-off".

Rockets and piggybacks

Since the Wright *Flyer*, many aeroplanes have needed help of one sort or another to get airborne. Some early jet aircraft, for example, had rockets attached to their underside which blasted the plane into the air. Other aircraft have been air-launched from a "mothership" – in the same way as the Bell X-1 – so they didn't have to lift off the ground under their own power at all. In the 1930s a bizarre piggyback aircraft, the Short-Mayo composite, was tried out. This was a seaplane carried into the air by a flying boat. The seaplane "took off" in the air from the flying boat's back.

Straight up

It was to avoid the need for runways that Vertical Take Off and Landing (VTOL) aircraft

WEIRD WORLD

US NAVY NIMITZ-CLASS CARRIERS, THE LARGEST WARSHIPS EVER BUILT, CAN HOLD MORE THAN 80 AIRCRAFT AND LAUNCH ONE OF THEM EVERY 20 SECONDS.

LOG ON...
www.AirAndSpaceMagazine.com/asm/web/site/QT.menu.html

were invented. The first of these were "tail-sitters" – aircraft like the Convair Pogo. This stubby, propeller-driven plane took off and landed with its nose pointing straight up into the sky, turning over into horizontal flight once airborne.

Unfortunately, a tail-sitter was murderously difficult to land. The pilot had to reverse the aircraft down while lying on his back with his feet above his head. It never caught on!

The Hawker Harrier, or "jump-jet", is much more successful. Developed in the 1960s, this plane takes off and lands on its wheels, as normal, but it also has jet nozzles that swivel. They point downwards to power the aircraft vertically into the air. Then they angle back for normal flight. The Harrier can perform a short, rather than vertical, take-off by setting the nozzles at an angle to fly from a short airstrip or a carrier deck.

All at sea

Taking off from an aircraft carrier creates all sorts of problems. However big the carrier, it can never provide the length of runway normally needed by a modern aircraft. The rolling and pitching of the carrier deck in a heavy sea doesn't help, either!

THE WINGS OF AN F-14 TOMCAT SWEEP BACK FOR SUPERSONIC FLIGHT. DURING TAKE-OFF AND LANDING, THEY OPEN OUT TO PROVIDE STABILITY AT LOW SPEED.

The carrier can turn into the wind so that its planes always have a headwind to provide lift. But catapults are still used to "kick-start" the aircraft, blasting them to about 225 kmh (140 mph) in under four seconds from standstill.

Hooked

The one task worse than taking off from a carrier is landing. Luckily, pilots can practise this manoeuvre on a flight simulator before trying it for real.

To stop the aircraft in time, carriers use arrester gear. This is a hook trailing from the tail of the aircraft which catches in a wire on the deck. It brings the plane to a dead halt within two seconds of touching down. The effect for the pilot is rather like driving into a brick wall!

Slow and steady

The key to landing an aircraft is being able to fly slowly enough. An aircraft designed to fly extremely fast may behave quite differently at low speeds. Coming in to land, an aircraft may lower flaps on the wing to

AN ARTIFICIAL HORIZON (LEFT) AND RADAR (ABOVE) IN THE COCKPIT HELP PILOTS FLY SAFELY EVEN WHEN THEY CAN'T SEE THE GROUND.

THE FLAPS ON A BOEING 747 ARE LOWERED IN READINESS FOR LANDING, ALONG WITH THE 16 MAIN WHEELS.

change the wing shape. A shape ideal for high-speed flight is turned into a shape that gives more lift at slower speed. Jet planes may also use a parachute, known as a drag chute or drogue, that unfurls from the tail to slow them down on the runway.

Flying blind

The main hazard when landing has always been poor visibility, caused by fog or thick cloud. As long ago as 1929, American pilot Jimmy Doolittle proved that it was possible to land an aircraft "blind". His cockpit had a hood over it so that he couldn't see outside. Inside he had instruments, such as an altimeter to tell him how high he was and an artificial horizon to show whether he was flying flat and level. He also had a radio to talk to a ground controller, and a radio navigation device to guide him to the airfield. Doolittle took off, flew around, and landed again without ever seeing where he was going.

Great modern gizmos

Aircrew nowadays have all the aids that Doolittle used, plus radar, on-board computers, and warning devices that, for example, tell them to "pull up" if they get too near the ground.

But pilots still very much prefer to be able to see where they're going when they come in to land. And most passengers still feel a tiny rush of relief when the wheels set down safely on the airport runway.

WEIRD WORLD

IT WAS NO FUN LANDING NAZI GERMANY'S KOMET ROCKET PLANE. THE WHEELS FELL OFF AFTER TAKE-OFF, AND THE PLANE LANDED ON BELLY SKIDS. THE JARRING IMPACT OFTEN BROKE THE PILOT'S SPINE.

WHIRLYBIRDS

An aircraft that can go straight up and down, stop in mid-air, or even fly backwards – that's the helicopter. It's hardly surprising that so many people – from traffic cops to rescue services, from soldiers to medics – have found it so useful. But making a helicopter that worked was even more difficult than getting a plane off the ground. It took years of experiment and bags of brain-power to create a whirlybird that didn't just whirl and whirl!

Speed isn't everything

In the 1920s, when new air speed records were being set every year, one aircraft was advertised proudly as able to fly slower than a man could run. The aircraft was the autogiro, and it was the brainchild of a Spanish inventor, Juan de la Cierva.

This odd-looking machine had an engine and propeller at the front, like any normal plane in those days. But above the pilot's head were rotating blades of the kind we're now used to seeing on helicopters. Some autogiros had little stubby wings, but they didn't really need them. It was the rotor that created the lift to get the aircraft into the air and keep it there.

Ancient technology

The fact that a rotating wing could fly had long been known. Since medieval times, children had played with spinning, flying toys – perhaps inspired by the flight of the winged seeds of sycamore trees.

All this meant that inventors of the Wright brothers' era knew two ways of getting air to flow over and under a wing to create lift. They could fix the wing to the aircraft and move the whole machine forward through the air – an aeroplane. Or they could move the wing through

THE HUGHES OH-6 CAYUSE WAS DESIGNED TO SERVE AS A SMALL, SPEEDY SCOUT IN THE VIETNAM WAR.

the air independently of the movement of the aircraft, by rotating it – a helicopter.

Up, but not away

In 1907, Frenchman Paul Cornu managed to hover above the ground for a few seconds, entering the record books for the first rotating-wing flight. But although his craft lifted briefly into the air, no one knew how to make such a machine fly around under the control of its pilot.

A SIKORSKY S-64 SKYCRANE LIFTS A COMPLETE PREFABRICATED HOUSE. SIKORSKY IMAGINED THE SKYCRANE MIGHT CARRY COMMUTERS TO WORK IN A DANGLING "POD", BUT IT NEVER HAPPENED.

Autogiros were the first successful rotating-wing aircraft, but they weren't true helicopters. There was no engine driving the rotor blades. The blades just spun freely, pushed around by the air as the autogiro flew forwards with its conventional propeller. Autogiros could fly very slowly, but they couldn't hover or fly backwards, as a helicopter can.

Out of control

Two big problems had to be solved before anyone could construct a helicopter that really worked.

First, it still wasn't possible to control a helicopter's flight.

The second problem was that as the rotor blades spun one way, their torque (twisting power) caused the helicopter's body to spin in the opposite direction.

Beating the spin

In the 1930s, helicopter makers found two different answers to the spinning problem. German Heinrich Focke – the man who differently. He fixed a small upright rotor to the tail of his VS-300.

This not only stopped the helicopter from going into a spin, but could be used to help steer the machine. Today, most helicopters use a tail rotor, Sikorsky-style, although some big helicopters have two main rotors, Focke-style. A less common third type have little jets at the ends of their rotor blades, which also solve the spinning problem (though only physicists understand why).

B lade technology

Learning how to control a helicopter so it could fly in every direction took a lot of experiments with rotor blades. Gradually, aeronautical engineers began to understand in detail how they worked.

They found out how to change the angle at

is usually credited with building the first true helicopter in 1937 – put two big rotors on the top of his machine, rotating in opposite directions. The clockwise spin of one cancelled out the anticlockwise spin of the other. In the United States, Russian-born Igor Sikorsky did it

JUAN DE LA CIERVA'S AUTOGIRO, A PLANE WITH A ROTOR, PAVED THE WAY FOR TRUE HELICOPTERS. AMATEURS STILL ENJOY FLYING AUTOGIROS TODAY.

A HELICOPTER DOES WHAT HELICOPTERS DO BEST, RESCUING A PERSON IN DANGER ON THE NORTHERN COAST OF CALIFORNIA.

6512

U.S. COAST GUARD

which the blades cut through the air to control the amount of lift they gave, so the aircraft would rise, hover, or descend.

They found out that you needed a separate control to tilt the whole main rotor, which gives you the thrust to go forwards and backwards or turn to either side. Meanwhile, the tail rotor acts like the rudder on an aeroplane, helping to steer the machine right or left. If this sounds complicated, it is! There's nothing simple about flying a helicopter.

Versatile craft

Although helicopters are much slower than aeroplanes, they're amazingly useful. They can take off or land wherever there's a helicopter-sized open space. They can land on top of a building if it has a flat roof, or even a large front lawn.

Even where they can't land, helicopters can hover and winch people up on a cable. Many shipwrecked

sailors owe their lives to helicopter air–sea rescue. Helicopters have also saved the lives of thousands of accident victims by ferrying them swiftly to hospital.

Take the weight

By the 1960s, some helicopters were powerful enough to carry 50 people. There were plenty of roles for heavy-lift helicopters such as the Sikorsky Skycrane.

LOG ON...
Learn more about
helicopters at www.helis.com

They could help build skyscrapers, for instance, lowering parts for construction workers to assemble. The Russian Mil V-12 became the world's helicopter weightlift champion in 1967 by lifting nearly 40,000 kg (90,000 lb) – equivalent to six elephants.

Medical and military use

In war, helicopters were at first mostly used to move troops around and carry wounded soldiers from the battlefield to receive urgent medical care.

In the 1960s, however, they went on the attack. Helicopters were built bristling with guns and rockets, capable of blasting enemy tanks or trucks. But these fearsome machines were still slow compared with aeroplanes. It's hard to make a helicopter fly even as fast as 250 kmh (156 mph).

The future

Designers dream of making a cross between a heli and an aeroplane, which could fly a lot faster.

They've built "tilt-rotors" – winged aeroplanes with propellers that can swivel to point upwards, turning into helicopter-style rotors. They've even made an experimental helicopter that turns into a jet plane. Its whirling rotor blade can be stopped in flight and locked in position to make – hey presto! – a fixed wing.

But none of these devices has yet worked especially well. Perhaps it's best in the end to accept that, for helicopters, slow is the way to go.

THE AH-64 APACHE ATTACK HELICOPTER CAN DIRECT GUNS, GUIDED MISSILES AND ROCKETS AT AIR OR GROUND TARGETS.

INTO SPACE

In just over 40 years, we have moved from the first human in space to the first space tourist paying for a trip into orbit. Patrolling the night skies are many satellites, unmanned orbiting spacecraft that help us predict the weather or make distant phone calls. But the most fascinating goal remains sending craft with humans on board to explore deep space – the final frontier.

To boldly go

Imagine being the first person to travel to outer space. You are squashed inside a small, round capsule perched on top of a massive rocket. The rocket engines ignite with a roar and you are lifted up into the sky,

The world's first spaceman

That was the experience of Soviet cosmonaut Yuri Gagarin, who carried out the first space flight on 12 April 1961, circling the globe in just over an hour and a half. He had achieved a feat that had long seemed

ONLY 12 PEOPLE HAVE WALKED ON THE SURFACE OF THE MOON

accelerating so fast that you are pinned back in your seat as if by great weights.

After a few minutes, though, the rocket booster falls away and you are in orbit around the Earth. You are weightless, alone in space, witnessing a spectacle that no one has ever seen before – the continents and oceans passing below you like the pages of a giant atlas.

impossible. Space travel had been seen as the stuff of science fiction, not science fact.

Defying gravity

In some ways, however, space flight posed a simpler problem to inventors than aeroplane flight. In the 1800s, French

THE SOVIET ROCKET *VOSTOK 1* LIFTS OFF TO SEND YURI GAGARIN (INSET) ON THE FIRST HUMAN FLIGHT INTO OUTER SPACE.

fantasy novelist Jules Verne had the idea of sending someone into space as a human cannon-ball, fired from a huge gun. This wasn't totally ridiculous.

What holds you to the ground is the pull of Earth's gravity on your body. If you were propelled by a sufficient upward force to overcome the pull of gravity, you would end up in space.

Impossible speed

During the early 20th century, scientists such as the American Robert Goddard showed how in theory you could get enough oomph – from a liquid-fuelled rocket, rather than a gun. Building such a rocket posed a challenge. The speed

an astronaut would need to reach to break free of the Earth's gravity was a staggering 40,000 kmh (25,000 mph).

Missile technology

The eventual breakthrough in rocket development came at a terrible cost. During World War II, governments spent vast sums of money on creating rockets for use as weapons.

The first really effective rockets were the Nazis' V-2 missiles, developed by Wernher von Braun in Germany during World War II. After the war, building on the Nazis' lead, the United States and its Cold War enemy the Soviet Union developed ever more powerful rockets, designed to attack distant cities. Scientists knew that the same rockets could be used to send objects into space.

MEN ARE SHOT TO THE LUNAR SURFACE IN A GIANT SHELL IN *A TRIP TO THE MOON,* A 1902 FILM BY GEORGE MELIES.

THE ANCESTOR OF ALL SPACE ROCKETS WAS THE V-2, BUILT AS A WEAPON BY THE NAZIS DURING WORLD WAR II.

Sputnik

In 1957 the Soviet Union launched *Sputnik 1*, the first satellite, into Earth's orbit. *Sputnik 1* was tiny – about twice the size of a football – and its only function was to circle the globe emitting a regular "beep" from its radio transmitters. But it marked the beginning of the space age.

United States to put a human into space. Both countries took fighter pilots and trained them to be astronauts (the American word) or cosmonauts (Soviet-style). They designed pressurized spacesuits and cabins to protect the space traveller outside Earth's atmosphere, and heat shields to stop the spacecraft from burning up as it reentered the atmosphere at high speed.

Before Gagarin's flight no one knew if it would all work – but it did, and for a while he was the world's most famous man.

SPACE VOYAGERS HAVE INCLUDED FROGS, CHIMPS, AND INSECTS

Later in 1957, the Soviets put the first living creature into space, the dog Laika. Sadly, Laika was not to return.

The race is on

After *Sputnik*, the race was on between the Soviet Union and the

THE DOG LAIKA WAITS TO BECOME THE FIRST EARTH CREATURE TO ENTER SPACE.

Kennedy's great goal

Americans were shocked that the Soviets had beaten them into space. The United States was never far behind – Alan Shepard became the first American in space in May 1961, less than a month after Gagarin. But being second was not the American way, and US president John F. Kennedy committed his nation to the goal of putting a man on the Moon

manoeuvre in space, dock one craft with another, and carry out "spacewalks".

The Soviets struggled to keep up. In 1964 they notched up another first – the first craft to carry a crew of three into space. But they had to send the

before the decade's end. It seemed an impossible challenge. To reach the Moon would need a more powerful rocket than to lift someone into orbit. Astronauts would also have to live in space for

long periods. In a series of space missions in 1965 and 1966, called the Gemini programme, US astronauts learned how to

ED WHITE MAKES THE FIRST SPACEWALK BY AN AMERICAN ASTRONAUT ON 3 JUNE 1965. IN HIS RIGHT HAND IS A "GUN" HE COULD FIRE TO MANOEUVRE IN SPACE.

threesome up without spacesuits, since their capsule was too small!

B ig blaster

By the end of 1967, the Americans had their moon rocket. At 3,000 tonnes the Saturn V launcher was the heaviest object ever to fly. It was also the most powerful flying machine ever built. When it took off from Cape Canaveral, it shook the surrounding land like an earthquake.

The Saturn V was built in three sections, each with its own set of rockets and fuel supply. As each section was used up, it fell away into space, and the next section took over. On top of the rocket were a Command and Service Module (CSM) in which the astronauts would enter the Moon's orbit, and a Lunar Module (LM) to descend to the Moon's surface.

At Christmas 1968, three astronauts orbited the Moon on board *Apollo* 8, sending back stunning images of Earth.

ON LATER MOON MISSIONS, ASTRONAUTS TRAVELLED IN THE LUNAR ROVER (SEEN HERE PARKED BESIDE THE LUNAR MODULE).

Moonshot

The Moon landing came on 20 July 1969. Astronauts Neil Armstrong and Buzz Aldrin descended to the Moon's surface in the LM, while Michael Collins stayed in lunar orbit aboard the CSM.

Watched by a large part of the world's population on TV, Armstrong and Aldrin planted an American flag and collected rock samples, before heading back to Earth. Americans went on to land another 10 men on the Moon before terminating the programme in 1972.

Reusable spacecraft

The Moon landings were a hard act to follow. However, the US space agency NASA went on to produce something in its way just as remarkable: the Space Shuttle.

From the start of the space age, people had dreamed of an aeroplane that flew into space and back. The Shuttle was not quite a "space plane", as it needed booster rockets to lift it into space. Still, it was truly reusable, gliding down to an airstrip after a space mission. Shuttle duties would include launching satellites and visiting space stations.

The programme suffered a tragic setback on 28 January 1986, when the Shuttle *Challenger* exploded after launch, killing all seven crew. But by 2001 three of the Space Shuttle craft had been safely in service for 20 years.

BLAST-OFF! TWO ROCKET BOOSTERS, FIXED TO A HUGE BROWN FUEL TANK, LAUNCH THE SPACE SHUTTLE INTO THE SKY.

Living in space

Beaten to the Moon, the Soviets turned their attention to space stations – laboratories in which scientists could study space at close quarters. The last station, *Mir*, launched in 1985, stayed in orbit for 16 years.

Life in space wasn't easy. Everything would float away in the gravity-free environment, even water. Space-station dwellers had to shower inside a bag to keep the liquid in. They even slept in sleeping bags tied to a wall. Keeping a sense of daily routine was hard, because dawn broke and the Sun set 16 times every 24 hours.

But long-term space living was survivable. Russian cosmonaut Valeriy Polyakov stayed on *Mir* for 14 months in a row in 1994–95, and American biochemist Shannon Lucid spent 188 days in orbit in 1996. By then, space exploration had become an international effort, although with the United States far in the lead.

Since 1995, Americans have been leading a team of 16 nations in a project even more ambitious than *Mir* – the International Space Station (ISS).

LOG ON...
Learn about space travel at http://spaceflight.nasa.gov/

Space tourism

Forty years after the first manned space flight only a tiny number of people had travelled beyond Earth's atmosphere. This seemed set to change when, in April 2001, American businessman Dennis Tito became the first space tourist, paying $20 million for a trip to the ISS. Another company was planning tourist trips to Mars. Clearly, the history of space flight had only just begun.

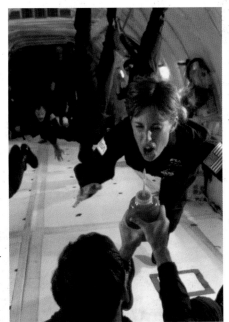

ASTRONAUTS TRAIN AT OPERATING IN A GRAVITY-FREE ENVIRONMENT. THEY ARE INSIDE A LARGE CARGO PLANE, WHICH CREATES WEIGHTLESS CONDITIONS BY FALLING STEEPLY – A BIT LIKE A FAIRGROUND RIDE.

EXTREME AIRCRAFT

Aircraft powered by the Sun, aircraft pedalled like bicycles, aircraft that fly at three times the speed of sound, aircraft that cruise at the speed a person can run – in their dazzling diversity, flying machines are wonders of the modern world. A century after the Wright brothers, inventors and adventurers are still busy pushing back the frontiers of flight.

Sky's the limit

With modern technical know-how, engine power, and new materials, there seems almost no limit to what a flying machine can be made to do.

Take the Lockheed SR-71 Blackbird. This was designed as a spyplane, meant to travel so high and fast over enemy territory that no fighter aircraft or missile could shoot it down.

Built in the 1960s, the Blackbird looks weird, with its sinister black paint (to help evade radar) and blade-like body. But its performance is even more amazing than its looks. For the

THE SR-71 SERVED AS AN AMERICAN SPYPLANE UNTIL THE 1990S. ITS POWERFUL CAMERAS COULD SPOT A GOLF BALL FROM 24 KM (15 MILES) UP.

76

THE ANGLO-FRENCH CONCORDE, THE WORLD'S ONLY SUPERSONIC AIRLINER, CAN FLY A MILE IN LESS THAN THREE SECONDS.

Blackbird can cruise at Mach 3 – over 3,200 kmh (2,000 mph) – at altitudes of over 25.5 km (16 miles).

Hot stuff

Flying at such speed makes the plane's skin very hot, through friction (rubbing) with the air. The Blackbird is mostly made of titanium alloy, a special metal that is light- and heat-resistant. Even so, when the aircraft lands after a mission its metal nose is often wrinkled by the heat. It has to be flattened out by ground staff using a blowtorch, much as you might iron a shirt!

Surprisingly, a speeding Blackbird is no gas-guzzler. When it flies flat out, air rushes through its engines so fast that the aircraft is propelled forward with hardly any need for the engines to burn fuel. This plane can virtually run on air.

Out of this world

Piloting an SR-71 Blackbird is an unforgettable experience. You travel faster than Earth's rotation, so if you fly westward at top speed, you see the Sun rise in the west, instead of setting there.

If you fly eastwards, adding the speed of the Earth's rotation to your own, you pass from day into night quite suddenly, like flying into a black curtain.

77

THE F-15
HAS BEEN
ONE OF THE
MOST SUCCESSFUL
OF ALL MODERN FIGHTERS,
COMBINING POWER WITH THE ABILITY FOR
HIGH-SPEED MANOEUVRES IN AIR COMBAT.

Since the 1970s, the experience of supersonic flight has no longer been restricted to trained aircrew. Anyone with enough cash to buy a ticket on Concorde can travel at twice the speed of sound.

Yet the airliner's passengers and crew travel at this awesome speed sitting in shirtsleeves, sipping cups of coffee. The only way you can tell you are moving fast is to feel the windows, which are hot from friction with the air.

What a blast!
For the real buzz of speed, nothing beats the experience of a modern jet-fighter pilot. A plane such as the F-15 can rise like a rocket to the height of Mount Everest (8,848 m, or 29,020 ft) in under a minute from take-off.

When the pilot ignites the afterburner, spraying fuel into the hot engine exhaust to go supersonic, the explosive kick is awesome! Or try skimming just above treetop height at about the speed of sound, the aircraft bucking as the autopilot makes it follow every dip and bump of the ground…

HIS OXYGEN MASK, HELMET, AND TINTED VISOR GIVE THE MODERN FIGHTER PILOT THE LOOK OF AN EXTRATERRESTRIAL ALIEN.

High stress
Fighter pilots wear a lot of special kit, and they need it because their aircraft can survive more strain than they can. In the days of aircraft made of canvas and wood, the risk of turning too tight and fast was that your aircraft might break up. In a modern fighter, the risk is that the pilot might lose consciousness – or worse.

WEIRD WORLD
MANY EXPERTS BELIEVE THAT FUTURE AIR WARS WILL BE FOUGHT WITHOUT PILOTS, AS FIGHTERS FLOWN BY COMPUTERS TAKE ONE ANOTHER ON IN UNMANNED COMBAT.

An aircraft such as the F-16 fighter is capable of fast, tight turns that would usually make a human pass out in seconds. Pilots fight back by donning "g-suits", like a pair of very tight shorts. These squeeze their lower body, forcing blood up to their chest and brain and helping raise their resistance.

Fighter pilots also wear helmets, oxygen masks, and sometimes also pressurized suits, like those worn by astronauts. It's a long way from the days when fliers liked to feel the wind in their hair!

The power of thought
Without computer wizardry, jet fighters would be unflyable. Everything happens too fast and is too complicated for any human to manage. But even with the help of computers and touch-of-a-button "fly-by-wire" controls,

fighter pilots find it ever more difficult to cope. An idea being seriously explored is to link the aircraft controls directly to the pilot's brain waves, so that the pilot simply "thinks" commands in order to fly the plane.

Giants of the airways

If some aircraft are remarkably fast, others stand out for their size. When a fully laden Boeing 747-400 jumbo jet lifts off from a runway, there's about 400 tons of aircraft, fuel, passengers, crew, and

luggage heading into the sky. The next generation of airliners threatens to dwarf this. The Airbus 380, set to make its debut at the world's airports in 2006, will weigh about 600 tonnes at take-off, with up to 550 passengers in its huge double-decker interior. How is it possible to move such massive weights around the sky, supported by thin air?

The simple answer is engine power. The Wright brothers believed that their invention would never work for large-scale airliners – they thought aircraft would always be light, flimsy "kites".

TO AN ENEMY'S RADAR THE STEALTH FIGHTER LOOKS NO LARGER THAN A SPARROW, THANKS TO ITS BIZARRE BODY SHAPE AND COLOUR.

The piston engines available in the Wrights' day were no more powerful than those in a small car or a motorbike. The engines of a jumbo jet are closer in scale to the engines that drive big ships. Given powerful enough engines, and using the same principles of flight that worked for the Wright brothers in 1903, plane designers can make almost any size of aircraft fly.

The B-2 stealth bomber, on the other hand, is all wavy curves, a "flying wing" with no fuselage at all.

The point of these shapes is to confuse enemy radar, and it works. Stealth planes can steal through air defences at night, invisible as ghosts. They're not an ideal shape for flying, but

LOG ON...
www.dfrc.nasa.gov/
gallery/photo/

Ghost planes

Today, you can also make an aircraft almost any shape you like. When designers in the 1980s were asked to create "stealth" planes, invisible to radar, they came up with some of the oddest-looking craft ever to fly.

The F-117 stealth fighter is all strange angles, so menacing in its black paint that it was nicknamed the "Bat Plane".

THE AIRBUS BELUGA, ONE OF THE BIGGEST OF ALL AIR TRANSPORTERS, CARRIES AIRLINER PARTS FROM ONE FACTORY TO ANOTHER.

that doesn't matter. Aircraft designers joke that engines and electronic control systems are now so good that, if they wanted, they could fly the Statue of Liberty.

WEIRD WORLD

THE COCKPIT GLASS ON STEALTH AIRCRAFT IS PAINTED WITH GOLD, WHICH BLOCKS RADAR PULSES. OTHERWISE ENEMY RADAR WOULD SPOT THE BACK OF THE PILOT'S HELMET THROUGH HIS HEAD!

Going the distance

However advanced aircraft have become, fliers always seem to find new challenges. In 1986, for example, Americans Dick Rutan and Jeana Yeager became the first people to fly non-stop around the world without in-flight refuelling – something none of the latest airliners or military planes could do.

Rutan and Yeager's propeller-driven plane, *Voyager*, was purpose-built from super-light materials. It flew for 42,212 km (26,382 miles) on the fuel it had been carrying at take-off. The round-the-world journey took nine days because *Voyager* travelled no faster than 176 kmh (110 mph) – any faster and it would have used up too much fuel. The intrepid pair spent those nine days and nights in a cockpit less than 60 cm (2 ft) wide. Luckily, they were good friends!

Pedal power

Even the dream of human-powered flight has at last been fulfilled. Scientists knew that humans could never fly by flapping their arms. But nobody said it couldn't be done by pedalling with your legs.

In 1977 a team in California built the Gossamer *Condor*, an aircraft that weighed next to nothing and had a

propeller turned by pedals like those on a bicycle. Cyclist Bryan Allen piloted the *Condor* around a figure-of-eight course 2.4 km (1.5 miles) long.

This first human-powered flight has since been followed by many more. In 1988, for

VOYAGER FLEW NON-STOP AROUND THE WORLD IN 1986. THOUGH LIGHT, IT HAD A LONGER WING THAN MOST AIRLINERS.

F ull circle

The same spirit of record-breaking and adventure-seeking brought a surprise comeback for ballooning, the earliest form of human flight.

In the 1990s, an epic contest developed to see who would be the first to fly a balloon right around the world. Using the jet stream, the strong winds that blow at very high altitude around the globe, balloonists were able to travel at speeds of well over 160 kmh (100 mph).

In March 1999 Bertrand Piccard and Brian Jones finally made it around the world in their balloon *Breitling Orbiter 3*, taking just under 20 days.

F eet on the ground

At the start of the 21st century, many of the most interesting new aircraft do without a pilot on board. An example is the Helios flying wing, which took to the air in 2001.

instance, Greek cyclist Kanellos Kanellopolos pedalled 118 km (74 miles) over the Aegean Sea between the islands of Crete and Santorini – the route said to have been taken by the mythical Daedalus. Pedal-powered craft aren't exactly useful, but who could resist proving it could be done?

83

Helios travels at only 32 kmh (20 mph), but with no need to refuel it can fly for months on end. In theory, it could stay in the air for ever, or at least until it fell apart. The craft is totally "green", using up no fossil fuel and creating no pollution. And it can fly at extreme altitudes approaching the edge of outer space.

Head in the clouds

But however useful unmanned aircraft are, the human urge to fly will never die. Every year more people take to the air, from hang-gliding enthusiasts leaping off cliffs to millionaires piloting their own private jets.

Now that humans have a taste for flight, no one will ever persuade them to leave the skies to the birds.

One of the strangest-looking aircraft ever, Helios is "piloted" by a controller on the ground. Its huge wing is covered in solar panels which use sunlight to generate the electricity to power its 14 motors. It stores surplus power during the day so that it can fly on through the night.

POWERED BY THE SUN, THE HELIOS FLYING WING TAKES OFF UNDER THE CONTROL OF ITS "PILOTS" ON THE GROUND.

REFERENCE SECTION

Whether you've finished reading *Flight*, or are turning to this section first, you'll find the information on the next eight pages really helpful. Here are all the aviation facts and figures, background details, and unfamiliar words that you might need. You'll also find a useful list of website addresses – so whether you want to surf the net or look for flight facts, these pages should turn you from an enthusiast into an expert.

HISTORIC MOMENTS IN FLIGHT

21 November 1783
The Marquis d'Arlandes and Pilâtre de Rozier make the first air journey in a Montgolfier balloon.

1809–10
Sir George Cayley publishes *On Aerial Navigation*, setting out the basic principles of heavier-than-air flight.

1852
Henri Giffard flies a steam-powered balloon, the first powered aircraft.

1890
Clément Ader's steam-powered aeroplane, the *Eole*, briefly lifts from the ground.

1900
The Wright brothers begin glider flights at Kitty Hawk, North Carolina, USA. Count Zeppelin builds his first airship.

17 December 1903
The Wrights achieve the first powered, sustained, controlled, heavier-than-air flight at Kill Devil Hills, near Kitty Hawk.

1904–05
The Wrights continue their flight experiments, staying airborne for over half an hour at a time.

13 November 1907
Paul Cornu achieves the first lift-off in a primitive helicopter.

January 1908
In Paris, Henri Farman flies a 1-km (0.6-mile) circuit in a Voisin biplane. The French hail this as the first true, heavier-than-air flight.

August 1908
Wilbur Wright flies in France. The Wright brothers are recognized as having been the first to fly.

25 July 1909
Louis Blériot is the first person to fly a plane across the English Channel.

August 1909
The world's first air show is held in Reims, France.

1910
Zeppelin airships begin the world's first air passenger service.

23 September 1910
Georges Chavez flies over the Alps, but is killed in a crash at the end of his flight.

1911
Cal Rodgers flies across the United States from coast to coast. Aircraft are used for the first time in war, by Italy against Turkey in Libya.

1914
Igor Sikorsky flies his four-engined aircraft *Ilya Muromets* a distance of 2,600 km (1,625 miles).

1915
In World War I, the first dogfights take place between rival fighter aircraft; Zeppelin airships conduct the first air raids on London.

21 April 1918
German air ace Manfred "Red Baron" von Richthofen is killed.

1919
The first regular airline services start up in Europe.

14–15 June 1919
John Alcock and Arthur Brown make the first non-stop flight across the Atlantic Ocean.

1921
American air commander Billy Mitchell stages the first sinking of a battleship by an aircraft.

1926
American scientist Robert Goddard makes the first liquid-fuelled rocket.
20–21 May 1927
Charles Lindbergh flies solo from New York to Paris.
1929
The airship *Graf Zeppelin* flies around the world in 21 days.
24 September 1929
James Doolittle makes the first "blind flight", using instruments alone.
1932
Amelia Earhart is the first woman to fly solo across the Atlantic Ocean.
1936
The Douglas DC-3 airliner appears. The Focke-Achgelis FW 61, the first practical helicopter, flies.
6 May 1937
The airship *Hindenburg* is destroyed by fire at Lakehurst, New Jersey.
27 August 1939
Flight of the first jet-powered aircraft, the Heinkel He 178.
August–October 1940
The Battle of Britain – the first battle fought in the air alone – takes place.
7 December 1941
Japanese carrier-borne aircraft bomb the US fleet at Pearl Harbor.
1944
The first jet aircraft fly in warfare. The Germans launch V-2 rockets against London and Antwerp.
14 October 1947
Chuck Yeager breaks the sound barrier in the Bell X-1 rocket plane.
1952
The world's first jet airliner, the De Havilland Comet, enters service.
November 1953
Scott Crossfield passes Mach 2 in the Douglas Skyrocket.

1958
The Boeing 707 jet airliner enters commercial service.
12 April 1961
Soviet cosmonaut Yuri Gagarin becomes the first person in space.
1965
American and Soviet crews make the first space walks.
1966
The Harrier V/STOL aircraft is successfully flown.
20 July 1969
Neil Armstrong becomes the first person to walk on the Moon.
1970
The Boeing 747, the first jumbo jet, enters commercial service.
1976
The supersonic airliner Concorde enters service.
23 August 1977
Bryan Allen makes a human-powered flight in the Gossamer *Condor*.
April 1981
The Space Shuttle enters service.
December 1985
Dick Rutan and Jeana Yeager fly around the world non-stop without refuelling in their aeroplane *Voyager*.
28 January 1986
The Space Shuttle *Challenger* explodes soon after lift-off.
1999
Bertrand Piccard and Brian Jones fly around the world non-stop in the balloon *Breitling Orbiter 3*.
2001
Helios remote-controlled, solar-powered flying wing flies.
April 2001
American businessman Dennis Tito becomes the first paying space tourist.

HEROES OF AVIATION

Clément Ader (1841–1925)
French engineer Ader made a steam-powered aeroplane that briefly lifted off the ground in 1890. When he built a more ambitious machine for the French Army, however, it would not fly at all.

Louis Blériot (1872–1936)
French businessman Blériot built the monoplane in which he crossed the English Channel in 1909. He later gave up flying as too dangerous, and manufactured aeroplanes instead.

Sir George Cayley (1773–1857)
Cayley carried out experiments with models and full-size gliders, and wrote a scientific description of the basics of heavier-than-air flight.

Bessie Coleman (1896–1926)
US flying schools would not accept an African American woman, so Bessie learned to fly in France. "Queen Bess" later became a famous stunt flier. Her ambition to open a black flying school was thwarted by her death in an air show accident.

Glenn Curtiss (1878–1930)
In 1909 this American former bike racer set a world air speed record of 75 kmh (47 mph) in France. He later made seaplanes and flying boats.

James Doolittle (1896–1993)
A stunt flier and racing pilot in the 1920s, Doolittle's feats included making the first "blind" flight and winning the 1932 Thompson

Trophy in a Gee Bee Racer. In 1942 he led a famous raid on Japan by carrier-launched B-25 bombers .

Amelia Earhart (1898–1937)
Earhart was the first woman to fly across the Atlantic, as a passenger, in 1927, and the first woman to pilot a plane across the Atlantic in 1932. She disappeared over the Pacific while trying to fly around the world.

Henri Farman (1974–1958)
Paris-born Farman made a number of record-breaking flights in 1908–09. He was the first man to fly a plane from one town to another. With his brother, Maurice, he became one of France's top aircraft manufacturers.

Anton Fokker (1890–1939)
Dutch-born Anton Fokker made fighter aircraft for Germany during World War I, including a triplane for Baron von Richthofen. After the war his company built airliners.

Howard Hughes (1905–76)
An eccentric millionaire who also made movies, Hughes became a leading pilot in the 1930s, setting a number of records. He built the largest aeroplane ever, the Hercules "Spruce Goose" flying boat, but it flew only once, in 1947.

Charles Kingsford Smith (1897–1935)
The most famous Australian flier, Kingsford Smith was the first to fly across the Pacific from America to

Australia in 1928 and founded Australian National Airways in 1929. He disappeared off Burma during an attempted England–Australia flight.

Otto Lilienthal (1848–96)
German engineer Lilienthal's trials with early gliders and his writings on bird flight had a profound influence on the Wright brothers. He was killed in a glider crash.

Charles Lindbergh (1902–74)
Lindbergh was a barnstormer and an air-mail pilot before winning fame for flying solo from New York to Paris in 1927. He made other pioneering flights, and promoted aviation in his native United States.

R. J. Mitchell (1895–1937)
English aircraft designer Reginald Mitchell worked for the Supermarine company. He designed the Spitfire fighter, as well as the seaplanes that won the Schneider Trophy.

Charles Nungesser (1892–1927)
Nungesser, a French air ace during World War I, scored 43 kills despite being injured in crashes. In 1927 he attempted, with François Coli, to fly from Paris to New York. They disappeared without trace.

Baron Manfred von Richthofen (1892–1918)
Known as the Red Baron, this German cavalry officer took up flying in 1915. Fighting in World War I, he scored 80 kills, leading other fighter pilots in "Richthofen's Flying Circus". He was shot down and killed in the last year of the war.

Igor Sikorsky (1889–1972)
Sikorsky began designing aircraft in Russia before 1914, including the multi-engined *Ilya Muromets*. Moving to the United States, he built flying boats before creating the pioneering VS-300 helicopter in 1939.

Sir Frank Whittle (1907–96)
In the early 1930s, Whittle, a Royal Air Force pilot, designed a turbojet air engine in his spare time. He won no official backing for it, and Germany was the first country to fly jets. The first British jet with a Whittle engine flew in 1941.

Orville and Wilbur Wright (1871–1948 and 1867–1912)
Born in Dayton, Ohio, the Wright brothers made bicycles before taking up flight experiments in 1900. By 1905 they had an aeroplane capable of substantial flights, demonstrating it in public in 1908. After 1910 they played little part in aviation.

Chuck Yeager (1923–)
Yeager joined the US Army Air Corps and flew Mustang fighters against Germany in World War II. After the war he became a test pilot, passing Mach 1 in 1947 and breaking other speed records into the 1950s.

Count Ferdinand von Zeppelin (1838–1917)
German aristocrat Count Zeppelin was more than 60 years old when his first airship, LZ1, flew in July 1900. He went on to become a national hero, living to see zeppelins used as bombers in World War I.

89

FLIGHT GLOSSARY

Afterburner
Device that sprays fuel into the rear nozzle of a jet engine where it ignites to create extra thrust.

Aeroplane
Heavier-than-air powered flying machine with a fixed wing or wings.

Airship
Powered, lighter-than-air aircraft.

Altimeter
Cockpit instrument that shows an aircraft's height above the ground.

Artificial horizon
Cockpit instrument that shows whether the plane is in level flight.

Assisted take-off
Take-off with the use of power from, for example, rockets or a catapult.

Autogiro
Aircraft with both a propeller and a helicopter-style rotor.

Automatic pilot (or autopilot)
Device that takes over some of an aircraft's controls from the pilot.

Barnstormer
Flier in the United States in the 1920s and 1930s who earned a living performing death-defying stunts.

Biplane
Aeroplane with two wings, one above the other.

Dirigible
Another word for an airship.

Drag
Force that holds back an aircraft as it pushes forwards through the air.

Fuselage
The body of an aeroplane, to which the wings and tail are attached.

Flying boat
Plane that can operate from water.

Glider
Heavier-than-air aircraft without an engine. It flies by riding on thermals (rising warm air flows).

Jet engine
Engine that creates forward motion by forcing hot gas out of a nozzle at the back.

Jumbo jet
Large, wide-bodied airliner such as the Boeing 747.

Lift
The upward force that helps a plane fly, generated by air passing more quickly over the wing than under it.

Mach number
Number used to show aircraft speed relative to the speed of sound – Mach 1 is the speed of sound.

Monoplane
Aeroplane with one wing.

Piston engine
Internal-combustion engine that, on an aircraft, powers a propellor.

Pitch
Movement of an aircraft's nose up or down (see *roll* and *yaw*).

Pressurized cabin
Aircraft interior that is kept at a comfortable air pressure even at high altitude, where air pressure is low.

Radar
Device for detecting distant objects by bouncing radio pulses off them.

Retractable undercarriage
Wheels that can be pulled up into an aircraft's fuselage or wings after take-off and lowered again for landing.

Roll
Tilting movement of an aircraft in which one wingtip rises and the

other falls (see *pitch* and *yaw*).

Rotating-wing craft
Helicopter or autogiro.

Seaplane
Aeroplane with floats for taking off from and landing on the water.

Sound barrier
The impossibility of reaching the speed of sound in an aircraft that is not designed for supersonic flight.

Stall
An aircraft is said to stall when low air flow over the wings (at very low speed) causes the plane to drop.

Stealth
Military technology that reduces an aircraft's visibility on a radar screen.

Stratosphere
One of the higher layers of Earth's atmosphere.

Supersonic
Faster than the speed of sound.

Thrust
Force that drives an aircraft or rocket.

Turbulence
Violent movement of air currents.

VTOL
Stands for Vertical Take Off and Landing, a term for planes such as the Hawker Harrier which need no runway.

Wind-tunnel
Device for testing aircraft designs by simulating the effects of flying.

Yaw
Movement of an aircraft's nose to right or left (see *pitch* and *roll*).

Zeppelin
German airship, especially one built by Count von Zeppelin's company.

GREAT AIRCRAFT

Wright *Flyer*
The first aeroplane to achieve sustained, powered flight, the Wright 1903 *Flyer* made only four flights, all on the same day. A biplane with a 12-hp engine, it reached 48 kmh (30 mph) over a maximum distance of 260 m (850 ft).

Bleriot XI
The monoplane in which Blériot crossed the English Channel in 1909 became one of the best-selling aircraft of its day. The original version, with a 25-hp engine, had a top speed of 58 kmh (36 mph). Later models fitted with 60-hp Gnome rotary engines were faster.

Fokker D7
A German biplane single-seat fighter from late in World War I, the Fokker D7 had a 185-hp engine and a top speed of 187 kmh (117 mph).

Ford Trimotor
This corrugated-metal monoplane airliner was introduced in 1926. With three 220-hp engines, the "Tin Goose" carried 15 passengers at up to 200 kmh (125 mph).

Douglas DC-3
The all-metal DC-3 entered service in 1936. It had two 1,200-hp engines and carried up to 21 passengers at 296 kmh (185 mph), crossing the

United States with two or three stops. By 1939 the DC-3 carried 90 per cent of the world's airline traffic.

Supermarine Spitfire
First flown in 1936, the Spitfire was one of a new generation of all-metal, single-seat monoplane fighters. With a 1,470-hp engine it could fly at over 560 kmh (350 mph) at altitudes of up to 11,130 m (36,500 ft).

B-17 Flying Fortress
The Americans used the Boeing B-17 to bomb Germany in World War II. It had a 1,816-kg (4,000-lb) bomb capacity and 10 crew, and carried up to 13 machine-guns in defence.

North American P-51 Mustang
One of the best late-World War II single-seat fighters, the Mustang reached 720 kmh (450 mph) and flew over 3,200 km (2,000 miles) without refuelling.

Messerschmitt Me 262
The first jet fighter, used by the Nazis in 1944–45, the Me 262 had two 8.8-kN (1,984-lb) thrust turbojet engines. It could reach speeds of 860 kmh (540 mph).

North American F-86 Sabre
Entering service with the US Air Force in 1948, the Sabre single-seat jet fighter saw action in the Korean War (1950–53).

Boeing B-52 Stratofortress
The B-52 was introduced in 1955. A giant jet bomber capable of delivering nuclear weapons, the Stratofortress was the mainstay of America's Strategic Air Command during the post-war Cold War era. It was still in service in 2002.

Boeing 707
The Boeing 707 was the first truly successful jet airliner. Introduced in 1958, it stayed in production until 1977. In the version with four 85-kN (19,000-lb) thrust turbofan engines the 707 carried 147 passengers a maximum of 8,000 km (5,000 miles) at about 970 kmh (600 mph).

MiG-21
The Soviet MiG-21 single-seat fighter flies at up to 2,220 kmh (1,390 mph). Introduced in 1959, it was still in service in 2002 with the Chinese Air Force.

Lockheed SR-71 Blackbird
First flown in 1962, the Blackbird spyplane flies at up to 3,600 kmh (2,250 mph), and operates at a maximum altitude of 30,500 m (100,000 ft). It remains the world's fastest winged jet aircraft.

Boeing 747
Introduced in 1969, the 747 was the first jumbo jet. It can carry 420 passengers about 10,880 km (6,800 miles) at 940 kmh (590 mph).

Aerospatiale/BAE Concorde
The world's only supersonic airliner, Concorde entered service in 1976. It can carry 128 passengers at up to 2,166 kmh (1,354 mph). After a crash in Paris on 25 July 2000, in which 113 died, the fleet was grounded until November 2001 while improvements were made.

FLIGHT WEBSITES

There are many websites detailing the history of flight. Some introduce the collections of aviation museums around the world.

www.allstar.fiu.edu/
Learn how engines work, and follow the history of flight from the earliest days, on this easy-to-follow aeronautical website.

www.dfrc.nasa.gov
Dryden Flight Research Center, formerly Edwards Air Force Base, has fascinating photos and videos of experimental aircraft.

www.first-to-fly.com
This "virtual" museum covers the work of the Wright brothers in some detail, but also has masses of information on the whole history of flight.

www.iwm.org.uk/duxford/index.htm
This website covers the Imperial War Museum's collection at RAF Duxford, UK. The airfield itself hosts regular air shows.

www.museumofflight.org
Among the collection at the Seattle Museum of Flight, in Washington State in the United States, are historic aircraft from the Boeing Company. They include the "Flying White House," the air transport of former US presidents.

www.nasm.si.edu/
The Smithsonian National Air and Space Museum, in Washington DC in the United States, is home to a spectacular collection of historic aircraft, as well as rockets and other spacecraft.

www.nlhs.com/hindenburg.htm
An American site run by the US Navy Lakehurst Historical Society covers the airship *Hindenburg* and its fiery end, as well as material on other airships.

www.rafmuseum.org.uk
The RAF Museum's collection at Hendon, London, UK, has more than 130 aircraft, including many from World War I and World War II.

www.wpafb.af.mil/museum
The US Air Force Museum in Dayton, Ohio, in the United States, has a huge array of military aircraft, and is home to the National Aviation Hall of Fame.

INDEX

CREDITS

Dorling Kindersley would like to thank: Chris Bernstein for the index; MSgt William Ackerman and Maj. Christopher Pirkl, 48th Fighter Wing, USAF; Katherine Boyce, RAF Museum, Hendon

---

The publishers would like to thank the following for their kind permission to reproduce their photographs:

Position key: a = above; b = bottom; c = centre; l = left; r = right; t = top

1: Aviation-Images.com/John Dibbs; 3: Aviation-Images.com; 4: The Flight Collection @ Quadrant Picture Library; 5: Aviation-Images.com/Mark Wagner; 6: Hulton Archive; 7: Aviation-Images.com/John Dibbs; 8: Science & Society Picture Library/Science Museum; 9: Corbis; 11: Science & Society Picture Library/Science Museum; 12–13: Science & Society Picture Library/Science Museum; 13: Science & Society Picture Library/Science Museum; 14–15: Hulton Archive; 15: Hulton Archive; 16: Hulton Archive; 16–17: Science & Society Picture Library/Science Museum; 17: Science & Society Picture Library/Science Museum. 18: The Art Archive br; 18–19: Science & Society Picture Library/Science Museum; 19: Science & Society Picture Library/ Science Museum; 20–21: Hulton Archive; 21: Hulton Archive/Edwin Levick; 22–23: Austin Brown/Aviation Picture Library; 22: Hulton Archive; 23: Corbis br; 24–25: Corbis; 25: Corbis tr; 26: Science & Society Picture Library/Science Museum; 26–27: Dominique Thirot; 28–29: Aviation-Images.com/Mark Wagner; 28: Science & Society Picture Library/Science Museum; 30–31: Corbis; 30: Hulton Archive bl; 32: Science & Society Picture Library/Science Museum; 33: Science & Society Picture Library/Science Museum; 34–35: Corbis; 34: Hulton Archive b; 36: Corbis c; 36: Mary Evans Picture Library b; 37: Corbis b, t; 38–39: Corbis; 39: Corbis tr; 40: Corbis t; 40–41: Corbis; 42: Mary Evans Picture Library; 43: The Flight Collection @ Quadrant Picture Library ca; Aviation-Images.com/John Dibbs c; 44: Aviation-Images.com/John Dibbs; 45: Corbis br; Aviation-Images.com/John Dibbs tr; 46: Aviation-Images.com/John Dibbs bl, c; 47: Aviation-Images.com/John Dibbs; 48–49: Corbis; 50: Science Photo Library; 51: Science Photo Library t; 52–53: Hulton Archive t; 53: Corbis b; 54–55: Aviation Images.com/John Dibbs c; 55: Aviation-Images.com/John Dibbs b; 56: Science & Society Picture Library/Science Museum c; 57: Corbis; 58; Corbis tl; 58–59: Corbis b; 60: Aviation-Images.com/ Mark Wagner b; 60–61: Corbis; 62–63: Corbis; 64–65: Hulton Archive t; 65: Hulton Archive b; 66: Corbis; 67: Corbis; 69: Science Photo Library main; Science Photo Library/Novosti tl; 70–71: Aviation-Images.com/Mark Wagner t; 70: Corbis/ Bettmann b; 71: Corbis b; 72–73: Corbis/ NASA; 73: Corbis/NASA b; 74: Corbis/ NASA; 75: Corbis; 76–77: Aviation-Images.com; 77: Corbis tr; 78–79: Corbis main image; 78: Aviation-Images.com/John Dibbs t; 80: Aviation-Images.com/Mark Wagner; 81: Aviation-Images.com/Mark Wagner; 82–83: Aviation-Images.com main image; 82: Corbis b; 84: Corbis Sygma/S. Feval tl; The Flight Collection/ NASA @ Quadrant Picture Library b; 86–87: Corbis; 88–89: Corbis; 90–91: Science & Society Picture Library/Science Museum; 92–93: Corbis.